LIFE SUCKS.

BY
AARON POSNER

SORT OF ADAPTED FROM
UNCLE VANYA BY ANTON CHEKHOV

★

★

DRAMATISTS
PLAY SERVICE
INC.

D1206299

NOTE ON BILLING
Anyone receiving permission to produce LIFE SUCKS. is required to give credit to the Author as sole and exclusive Author of the Play on the title page of all programs distributed in connection with performances of the Play and in all instances in which the title of the Play appears, including printed or digital materials for advertising, publicizing or otherwise exploiting the Play and/or a production thereof. Please see your production license for font size and typeface requirements.

Be advised that there may be additional credits required in all programs and promotional material. Such language will be listed under the "Additional Billing" section of production licenses. It is the licensee's responsibility to ensure any and all required billing is included in the requisite places, per the terms of the license.

SPECIAL NOTE ON SONGS/RECORDINGS
Dramatists Play Service neither holds the rights to nor grants permission to use any songs or recordings mentioned in the Play. Permission for performances of copyrighted songs, arrangements or recordings mentioned in this Play is not included in our license agreement. The permission of the copyright owner(s) must be obtained for any such use. For any songs and/or recordings mentioned in the Play, other songs, arrangements, or recordings may be substituted provided permission from the copyright owner(s) of such songs, arrangements or recordings is obtained; or songs, arrangements or recordings in the public domain may be substituted.

For all my old friends, who taught me so much.
And for all my old friends, who didn't teach me nearly enough.
And for all my other old friends, too…
For all the amazing theatre artists I work with all the time,
who always make my work so much better,
and to whom I am deeply and eternally grateful…
And mostly for my wife, Erin, and my daughter, Maisie,
who are my guides, my joys, my loves…and my bright
beacons in an all too often murky world.

THANK YOUS

Ari Roth.

Howard Shalwitz.

Erin Weaver.

Andy White.

Theater J.

Lookingglass Theatre.

And all the actors and designers and technicians from the Theater J and Lookingglass productions.

LIFE SUCKS. was first produced by Theater J (Adam Immerwahr, Artistic Director; Rebecca Ende Lichtenberg, Managing Director) at the Aaron and Cecile Goldman Theater in Washington, D.C. It was directed by Aaron Posner; the composer and sound designer was James Sugg; the lighting design was by Nancy Schertler; the set design was by Meghan Raham. The cast was as follows:

VANYA .... Sasha Olinick
SONIA .... Judith Ingber
ELLA .... Monica West
BABS .... Naomi Jacobson
THE PROFESSOR .... John Lescault
DR. ASTER .... Eric Hissom
PICKLES .... Kimberly Gilbert

The Midwest premiere of LIFE SUCKS. was produced by Lookingglass Theatre Company (Heidi Stillman, Artistic Director; Rachel E. Kraft, Executive Director) in Chicago, Illinois. It was directed by Andrew White, the sound designers were Chris LaPorte and Andre Pluess; the scenic and lighting design was by Brian Sidney Bembridge; the stage manager was Patia Bartlett. The cast was as follows:

VANYA .... Eddie Jemison
SONIA .... Danielle Zuckerman
ELLA .... Chaon Cross
BABS .... Barbara E. Robertson
THE PROFESSOR .... Jim Ortlieb
DR. ASTER .... Philip R. Smith
PICKLES .... Penelope Walker

CHARACTERS

VANYA—45. A ruminator. A kvetch. A smart, sweet, passionate, insightful, wound-tight failure.

SONIA—24. Kind, caring, and quirky. Serious self-esteem issues. Not comfortable in her body.

ELLA—36. Searching, frustrated, hopeful, and sad. Very attractive and rampantly desirable.

BABS—64. Vibrant, artistic, outspoken, and even enlightened. A great soul and scrappy wit.

THE PROFESSOR—62. Big mind, big ego, big vocabulary, small-ish soul. Selfish. Well-meaning.

DR. ASTER—52. Broken, beautiful, dissatisfied, savvy, and sad. He cares deeply and oddly.

PICKLES—40ish. An odd, sweet, loyal duck. Very literal. A relentlessly positive utopian lesbian.

SETTING

The world should be a fairly simple, flexible space with multiple areas so that more than one thing can be happening at the same time. There should be space for actors to be when they are not "onstage" or the center of attention but where they can still be (at least partially) seen. The space should feel open, practical, and yet theatrical and even Chekhovian in some way. Since the play is about Love and Longing, that could be reflected in the setting somehow.

THE ACTING STYLE

Aggressively honest. Achingly transparent. Always reaching and striving for the best way to express whatever fucked up, painful, wonderful thing needs to be expressed at the moment. Heartfelt, but never sentimental; odd (quirky, even), but never cute or clever or cloying; fast and front-footed, but never rushed; full of endless AMAZEMENT and WONDER; and always, always, always tipping toward more love, more hope, more passion and more perseverance.

THE ACTOR/AUDIENCE RELATIONSHIP

The characters are always the characters. They are never the actors. The characters are fully invested in the realities of their world and the web of relationships in which they are so deeply entangled… but they also know they are in a play! They know the audience is right there and that reality never leaves them. They don't need to acknowledge the audience all the time, but they are always there to be included and engaged if the actor so desires.

TECHNICAL TEXT NOTES

/ indicates that the next person starts speaking there…

* on either side of a word or phrase means that that line or word should be tailored specifically to the actual actors playing the roles in that given production…

LIFE SUCKS.

The Launch: Love & Longing!

The cast comes on. They talk to the audience...

VANYA. Okay, so...

SONIA. Here we go!

BABS. *(Not without irony...)* More art!

PICKLES. *(À la* Fantasy Island...*)* Look boss! The play! The play!

VANYA. *(Already mildly annoyed by her...)* C'mon, please...

ASTER. So, yeah, right, well...

ELLA. Thanks for coming.

BABS. We're the *actors.* And you, of course, are the *audience.*

PICKLES. We couldn't do this without *you.* I mean, think about it. Without you, we'd have a kind of... "one hand clapping" situation.

> *They all ponder that...*

VANYA. I don't even know / what that

PICKLES. Or, I guess, more like NO hands clapping. I mean, without you it's like we don't / even exist.

VANYA. *(To Pickles, gently, but seriously...)* Shhhh...

ASTER. Right, so... Cell phones off. Exits there and there, no photography or recording, blah blah blah. You all know these things, right?

PROFESSOR. Our play transpires in four succinct acts...just like Chekhov's original, superior play. We'll take an intermission between Acts Two and Three.

BABS. And if *you* won't unwrap things *really slowly* thinking we'll hear them less that way, then we won't either. I'm not sure why we seem to think if other people can't see us, they can't hear us either, but…*it's not true.* So, if we can just save loud candies till intermission or after the show that'd be terrific.

SONIA. Shakespeare calls his plays our "two hours' traffic on the stage…", and while we might / not be able—

ELLA. This one might be a bit more like two hours stuck in traffic…

SONIA. That's not / what I was going to say…

VANYA. Most of it is going to be about love and longing. Yep. That's right, campers. *LOVE.* And *LONGING.*

SONIA. That's not *all* it's about.

VANYA. Pretty much. So you can't say you weren't / warned.

ASTER. Well, this is off to a lovely start…

PROFESSOR. It's also about the audacious, ludicrous, and protean nature of the obstreperous and ever-feckless human heart.

PICKLES. *(Amazed by his pretentiousness…)* Holy Toledo, Batman…

SONIA. It's also about not getting what you want.

ELLA. Yes. Or getting what you thought you wanted but then… you know…

PICKLES. Or the opposite of all that.

BABS. *(A possibility…)* Or the inverse.

PROFESSOR. *(With deep insight…)* Or the *contra positive.*

VANYA. What does that even mean?

ASTER. It's also about how disastrously, irretrievably fucked up the world is, and the insanity of the choices we humans have made for the last four hundred years.

SONIA. Right…

VANYA. Right. That too.

BABS. *(Dropping in…)* And about *loss.*

    Beat. They all take that in…

VANYA. Yeah, well, so if you *aren't* interested in love and longing and loss…

ASTER. *(Reminding him of his perspective…)* Ummm…

VANYA. …and how fucked up the world is…then you may have, you know, *chosen your night's entertainment badly.* And you can actually leave right now if you want and you'll get a full refund for your ticket. Plus a dollar for your trouble.

BABS. You can probably catch *Mary Zimmerman's production of *Wonderful Town* at the Goodman.* I've heard really great things…

PICKLES. But thanks for coming…!

VANYA. Or going…

BABS. Oy vey…   ASTER. Really, Vanya?

VANYA. So, okay, let's get this *fakokta* thing started…!

    Folks head offstage or into positions to begin…

SONIA. *(To us, in confidence…)* Seriously, it's not that bad. Vanya's just…Vanya.

Anyway, you'll see. This is our play.

It's called LIFE SUCKS.

Thanks for coming.

Okay. Everyone ready?

Okay, then, off we go…!

ACT ONE: ALL THE PEOPLE

1.0 Work

Aster and Babs are talking. She drinks very small glasses of vodka. He is clearly a bit agitated and distracted. He looks offstage surreptitiously from time to time in the direction the walking party will eventually enter from...

ASTER. You know what my problem is? Do you?

BABS. *(She's thinking...)* Ummm...

ASTER. You know what my fucking problem is?

BABS. Astound me...!

ASTER. I work too hard.

BABS. Oh. *(Looking off where the others are walking.)* I thought you meant—

ASTER. *(He misses her point...)* I work way too fucking hard. (Sorry, Babs...)

BABS. (Oh, I don't care...)

ASTER. People are always, let's go here or let's do this or why don't you take a little break and I'm always, no no no, I can't, I can't, I've gotta *work*. That's what I say, constantly. "Gotta *work*." Like the world'll fucking end if I / don't *work*.

BABS. You swear too much.

ASTER. It's true, I do.

BABS. You do.

ASTER. You drink too much.

BABS. You're right, I do.

ASTER. We are none of us perfect.

BABS. You *do* work too much.

ASTER. I know!

BABS. But I / don't think—

ASTER. And to what end? I don't have, you know, a wife…or *children*. And even if I did, money screws kids up nine times out of eleven— *(To the audience…)* don't google it, I made it up, but still…cool, sane rich kids are the total exception and we all know it.

BABS. Want another drink?

ASTER. No. I have to go. I gotta wo—Did you hear that? It's ridiculous! I can't stop myself. Like some absurd machine… "Gotta work. Gotta work. Gotta work." And do you think people in 100 years will care how hard we worked? A few great geniuses, maybe, or an artist or two… But most of us? The normal people. Will anyone care? Not a chance. But still…!
And do you know what's even crazier than working so hard?

BABS. Enlighten me!

ASTER. You know what I do on those rare occasions when I'm not working.

BABS. You count groundhogs! Or…grouse, or…?

ASTER. Well, yeah, *that*, I do do that, but that's not crazy, that's the one sane thing I do, that's my work for the nature conservancy and… *(Fully realizing what she said.)* Hey, I'm not counting *grouse*, I'm tracking patterns of population and—

BABS. What's the crazier thing?

ASTER. Sorry?

BABS. You said you did something crazier than wasting your life working so much. So now, you know…I'm just dying to know what that could be.

ASTER. I work out. For hours. Sweat my ass off picking stuff up… and putting it down again. Picking it up, putting it down. Picking it up, putting it down, picking it up, putting it down, picking it up, putting it down, picking it up, putting it down, picking it up, putting it down… Pushing on things! And pulling on things! And *running in place*—for hours! There cannot be anything more ridiculous in modern life than a treadmill. You ever imagine what an alien would think if the first place they saw was a gym. Or worse, some ridiculous doctor in his own little living room just running in place for *hours*

13

and not getting anywhere. Not generating energy...*using it*! The fucking thing has to be plugged in! *(Bottom line.)* It costs me money to run with all my strength to get *nowhere*!

BABS. You, my friend... You, my dear, dear, dear one, *you* are the thing that's ridiculous. Do you even know what you're really complaining about?

ASTER. Ummm...

     Babs looks out the window at Ella, and back at Aster...

BABS. You and Vanya both. Just *ridiculous*...

1.1 Vanya

VANYA. *(Entering awkwardly.)* And speaking of ridiculous...!

ASTER. Oh, hey.

VANYA. Where are they?

ASTER. Walking...

BABS. "Perusing the garden on a postprandial perambulation..."

VANYA. Did he really say that?

BABS. Damn near...

VANYA. What a putz...

BABS. Methinks our dear old friend "The Professor" hath a lean and hungry eye...

VANYA. I'm sorry?

BABS. Never mind...

ASTER. What are you wearing?

VANYA. *(Looking at himself...)* What? They're clothes...

ASTER. I didn't know you owned a tie...

VANYA. Ha ha...

ASTER. Or...*cologne?*

BABS. *(Referring to the smell.)* Is that what that smell is?

VANYA. *(To Babs.)* Did *everyone* go?

ASTER. Yes, Ella went, too.

VANYA. *(Realizing he's been nailed...)* Shut up.

ASTER. *(An old, comfortable pattern...)* No, *you* shut up.

VANYA. *(Playful, but true, too...)* No, seriously, shut up...!

BABS. Oh, my God, you two...

ASTER. He started it.

VANYA. What do you mean "a lean and hungry eye"?

BABS. It's Shakespeare.

VANYA. I know that! But why did you say it?

BABS. I don't know. He just looks...

ASTER. What?

BABS. *Predatory* or something, I dunno... I never know what's going through that twisty little mind of his. I like him, I do, he's great for an annual game of Celebrity or Trivial Pursuit, but I trust him about as far as I can throw him.

VANYA. I'd like to throw him about as far as I can...trust him...

ASTER. Good one.

VANYA. You know what I mean.

ASTER. You mean you hate his fucking guts.

BABS. (Not to put too fine a point on it...)

VANYA. I can't believe I used to think he was *brilliant*. I'd sit at his knee, practically, and just listen to him drone on and on and on about art and music and, you know, Buddhism and Symbolism and veganism and any other -ism he was into at any given time, and I read all the books he told me to read until—

ASTER. Until what? I've never quite—

VANYA. Until I realized he was utterly full of shit, that he only really understood about a fifth of everything he talked about and that—I mean, fuck, I can hurl nine-dollar words around, too, you know... Why, I could profess it is not calumny, but rather axiomatic to aver that he's a scrofulous, vapid, orotund ass with inchoate, noisome notions, and a penchant for sesquipedalian elocution.

BABS. Wow. That was good...

VANYA. Or I could just call him a pedantic prick and be done with it.

ASTER. And you came to this conclusion…about the time he and Ella got married?

VANYA. Hey. Shut up.

ASTER. I'm just saying…

VANYA. The truth is I have ten times as much imagination and insight and and and…*understanding of the fucking universe* as he does, and yes, okay, yes, if Ella could see past my *tie* and my… *nerdy wimpishness* and my…*whatever*, and just see me for who I *really am*—and who he really is!—then she'd pack her bags, catch the first bus out of Dodge, and show up on my door step!

ASTER. Didn't you introduce them?

VANYA. So…help me out here, which word in Shut. Up. don't you understand?

ASTER. Ummm…

1.2 Topsy-Turvy

The Professor, Pickles, Sonia, and Ella enter from a walk.

PROFESSOR. It's a lovely garden now, Sonia, lovely. I mean, not astonishingly, *movingly* lovely like Switzerland, like those practically incandescent meadows near the base of the Tschingelhorn in the Bernese Alps, but lovely all the same…

SONIA. Thanks. I think…

PICKLES. It's sometimes hard to tell if you are complimenting us or insulting us…

PROFESSOR. *(Cheerily…)* Isn't it?

ASTER. The…*Shingelhorn*…?

PROFESSOR. *Tschingelhorn.* With a "*tsch*" at the beginning…

ASTER. I've always wanted to go to Switzerland.

PICKLES. I love that name. Alps. *Alps.* Sounds like a…cockney puppy. *(Barking it out…)* Here, Alps! Alps! Alps!

    Quick beat…

PROFESSOR. Ella, remember that couple we met at the Tschingelhorn? That terribly skinny ophthalmologist with the enormous mole...

ELLA. ...gynecologist...

PROFESSOR. ...on his face. Oh, yes, gynecologist. Not ophthalmologist?

ELLA. No.

PROFESSOR. Climatologist? I feel almost sure / that he—

ELLA. No. I know the difference between an eye, a vagina, and a hurricane.

> Beat.

ASTER. I feel almost certain there's a joke in there somewhere...

ELLA. Oh. Can you find it?

ASTER. I'm looking...

ELLA. Well go on... *(Prompting him...)* vagina, vagina, vagina...

PROFESSOR. Yes, well, Gynecologist. As the poet says: *Instabilis est memoriae amici.* Anyway, I swear, you could not have a conversation / with this man

VANYA. What does that mean?

PROFESSOR. Sorry?

VANYA. What does that *mean*? You know none of us speak Latin, why / would—

PROFESSOR. "The memory is a fickle friend." It's from Virgil.

VANYA. Then why the hell didn't / you just say...

PROFESSOR. Anyway, you could NOT speak with this...person...

VANYA. *(Overlapping.)* ...isn't language designed to communicate, not to...

PROFESSOR. without staring right at this incredible mole. I swear, it was not humanly possible. And he had a stutter, which I'm sure he developed in response to people staring at his...m-m-m-monolithic m-m-m-mole whenever he talked.

ELLA. *(She's been thinking...)* Maybe he was a *derma*tologist...

PICKLES. Oh, I've never been anywhere...

17

PROFESSOR. Well, you must go!

PICKLES. Where?

PROFESSOR. Anywhere! Travel! It's the only thing!

VANYA. Fascinating. An hour ago you said erudition was the only thing. Last night you said a great macchiato was the only thing. How many / only things…

PROFESSOR. Did someone say something? I heard a buzzing…a / gnat or…a fly or a…

VANYA. Yes, ha ha, very funny, very witty ha ha ha…

PROFESSOR. Travel is *enlightening*. It lets you know who you are and what really matters. You can never really understand where you are until you leave.

VANYA. And you understand, do you? Where you "are"?

PROFESSOR. I believe I do, yes.

VANYA. Where the hell are you, then? No, seriously, I really want to know. Where are you? From what great height do you presume to pontificate and / lecture us

PROFESSOR. *(Beating the air…)* There it is again, that annoying gnat…

VANYA. I'm serious, we've been listening to you hold forth for / all these years and I

ELLA.	SONIA.	PICKLES.
Oh, please please please, just stop it…	Uncle Vanya, please don't…	I think it was just a joke…

VANYA. All right. Down, boy, down! Heel! I mustn't talk, never ever talk!

BABS. *(Pleasantly.)* You've really become quite a pompous old shit, haven't you?

PROFESSOR. Oh, yes, yes…or so my friends are fond of telling me…

BABS. *(A friendly, positive toss-away…)* Perceptive friends.

PICKLES. Well, I thought that was a lovely walk.

BABS. Oh?

PICKLES. I should walk more. Just…*walk*…

ASTER. Did you enjoy your walk, Ella?

ELLA. Oh yes, yes. *(Mildly ironic...)* Spectacular.

PICKLES. You know, walk all over the land, and just...look at things...and see what's out there in the wide, wide world, you know?

Beat... Beat...

VANYA. How is it, Pickles, that nothing you say ever...*leads anywhere*? You speak, I hear you, it's perfectly reasonable and all, but I never have anything to say in return. And neither does anyone else. You're a conversation annihilator!

Quick, awkward beat...

PICKLES. Well...I am the Walrus. Coo coo cachooo...

Beat. Everyone just looks at everyone else...

ELLA. Well, I'm going to take a nap.

PROFESSOR. *(Pretend sotto voce.)* That's code for "I'm bored."

ELLA. It's not code, and I'm not bored, I'm just...*a tad weary.* The more I sleep these days, the tireder I seem to get. I'll be in bed if anyone needs me...

That image has the intended/unintended effect on the room... Aster looks out the audience and mouths "holy shit" as Ella leaves...

PROFESSOR. Well, back to work. See you all for dinner if I don't die in the meantime. I'll leave now so you can all talk about my wife behind her back...

He leaves...

BABS. I'm gonna get back to work, too. I'll be in my studio...

She leaves...

VANYA. *(To Sonia.)* What the hell are they really doing here?

SONIA. *(Back to Vanya.)* I don't know

VANYA. How long are they staying?

SONIA. I have no idea.

VANYA. You have no idea why they're here, or...

SONIA. No. He just said they were coming and could they stay a bit...

VANYA. Oy...

SONIA. I'll be back soon.

VANYA. Where are you going?

SONIA. Shopping. We need something for dinner. And she needs more flavored fizzy water.

> *Sonia leaves... Vanya, Aster, and Pickles are left standing there... They are all still in Ella's spell in their own particular manner...*

1.3 Ridiculous

VANYA. Oh my God, it's ridiculous...

PICKLES. What is?

VANYA. The air seems to just...leave the room with her when she goes...

PICKLES. *(Confused, as she is still thinking about Ella.)* Who, Sonia?

VANYA. No, you idiot... Ella.

PICKLES. Oh. *Yeah...*

ASTER. She does...*draw the eye.*

VANYA. Like a light has been turned off somewhere.

> *Pickles looks around to see what light, for a moment...*

ASTER. How long have they been married?

VANYA. Oh, God, I don't know. Eight years. Six. Nine. I don't know...

PICKLES. She isn't even really that pretty, really. I mean—she's *pretty* and everything...but she's not even really *that pretty*, you know...?

ASTER. She's very...

PICKLES. Yeah

VANYA. She's making me crazy.

ASTER. *(Smiling. Clearly reaching way, way back...)* Like whatshername...

VANYA. Who?

ASTER. Whatshername. Who lived on…umm…Agate Street?

VANYA. Lyn Burger?

ASTER. No! With the accent…and the "ducky waddle baby butt"?

VANYA. Ellie…! *(Jesus, how do you remember / what we called…)*

ASTER. Yeah, right, Ellie Petropolis, Jesus…

PICKLES. *(Coming off of looking at her…and alluring, still…)* Like a smoothie.

VANYA. What?   ASTER. What?

PICKLES. She reminds me of a smoothie.

ASTER. Huh.

PICKLES. Or an ocelot.

VANYA. What the hell are you talking about?

PICKLES. No, seriously. Like the World's Sexiest Ocelot…

ASTER. That's good. That's close, I think. *(Trying it out…)* A really sexy ocelot…

VANYA. Well, she's making me batshit crazy.

ASTER. Is she faithful?

VANYA. To what?

ASTER. To him.

VANYA. Why?

ASTER. No reason.

VANYA. What do you care?

ASTER. I don't. But is she?

VANYA. How should I know? It's hard to imagine, though. I mean… look at him!

PICKLES. What about him?

VANYA. He's awful! So absurdly…*self-obsessed.* Like the rest of us are beneath his notice. Like while he's talking to you he's really looking in a mirror.

PICKLES. Huh. I think he's really smart.

VANYA. You know what he teaches? You know what his *specialty* is in his rarified little enclave of academic elitism and self-aggrandizement?

ASTER. No, actually. You always just call him The Professor, so I don't—

VANYA. Ironically! You get that right?! I call him The Professor IRONICALLY!

ASTER. Yes, of course. But still…

VANYA. Semiotics. Semiotics!

PICKLES. That's the study of…big trucks?

VANYA. Signs! Symbols! Clues! It's the study of *clues*!!!

PICKLES. My bad…

VANYA. I mean…*why*? Who gives a fuck? I have a sign for him: STOP! Stop "studying" things that no real person in the real world could ever *imagine* caring about! At least esoteric sciences can lead to…you know…new kinds of *wheat* or or or or or better drugs or windmills or whatever, but Christ On A Cracker, endless impassioned arguments about—look, I stole this article he wrote from his room to try to get some…here…here… "Semiotic Phenomenology & The Relational Constitution of Presence" HELLO?!?!? Oh, and wait, there's a subtitle, thank God, this will really clear things up: "Thematizing the Problematic through Human Speech Praxis"

PICKLES. Practice?

VANYA. No! Praxis!

PICKLES. *(Meaning "that's so weird and problematic"…)* Hrghh…

VANYA. I mean…WHAT THE FUCK DOES THAT EVEN MEAN?!?!

PICKLES. Presence? Or Presents…?

Beat.

VANYA. What?!?

PICKLES. I'm saying, Presence, like…being here in this room… Or Presents, like…wrapped up for Christmas with a bow?

Beat.

VANYA. What possible difference does it make?!?!

PICKLES. Umm… They're / completely different…

VANYA. It's a vast conspiracy that costs real people gazillions of dollars each year. *Academics!* Privileged, arrogant fuckers arguing endlessly about esoteric minutiae so *stunningly meaningless* and *rampantly unimportant* that even they could not possibly care themselves, except that if they ever told anyone how little they cared they couldn't continue the absurd conspiracy of getting generations of over-privileged eighteen-year-old sparrow-farts to pay them and praise them and give them tenure and spend their time and our money arguing endlessly about…"The Phenomenology of Whatever-The-Fuck" and giving each other awards and making the rest of us feel like uncultured boobs and morons because we don't give a shit!

    Pause…

PICKLES. So you're not a big fan of his work?

VANYA. Shut up.

ASTER. So, I take it you're saying she *is* faithful to him.

VANYA. Yes, I think so. Which is another absolute horror in and of itself.

ASTER. Her *fidelity*?

VANYA. Yes. Absolutely. It's morally repugnant. It's against nature. It's like—

PICKLES. No.

VANYA. *(Taken aback…)* I'm sorry?

PICKLES. No. That's not right. Fidelity is *fidelity*. It's constancy. It's a commitment and it's to be honored, not mocked. Not *mocked*. You all make fun of me and I get it, I do, I guess I'm a little ridiculous, and maybe I'd make fun of me too if I were someone else, but I know about fidelity, / and I…

VANYA. Oh, God, Pickles, I'm not talking / about your…

PICKLES. I gave her my heart. I gave her my whole heart and we made each other a vow and I have been true to that vow / because

VANYA. But that was twenty years ago…!

PICKLES. Seventeen.

VANYA. Whatever. *(A throw-away…)* I'm not doing this again…

PICKLES. *(Turning abruptly to us in the audience instead...)* Iris was the love / of my life and, yes, she left me seventeen years ago, and

VANYA. Don't just tell *them*, that's not fair...!

PICKLES. everyone is always saying to me—move on. "It's time to move on." That's the exact phrase that everyone uses, like some agreed-upon plan: "It's time to Move On!"

VANYA. Because it is!   ASTER. It really is...

PICKLES. But here's the thing: I can't. I can't "move on." How can I? Because that love is still there. It still sits...right *there. (Pointing at her heart or gut or soul...)* I don't know how you all *(And she is talking simultaneously to the other actors and the audience...)* can just go from one lover to another to another to another, I don't, not if that love is real. Not if it's *real*. Love is love and it stays forever. I think. I think it stays *forever*.

VANYA. No one is saying—   ASTER. I don't think—

PICKLES. I don't even know what people mean when they say "Oh, yeah, we really loved each other back then..." or "Yeah, I *used* to really love her" 'cause I just think: Where did that love go? *Where did that love go???* Because I don't know about you, but I still love everyone I've ever loved.

Everyone I've ever loved, I still love.

> *She starts crying right about here...*

And I think I always will. The truth is...I don't know how to stop. And...and the other truth is... I don't *want* to stop.

My love for Iris is real.

And I don't want to move on.

I'm just fine where I am, thank you very much. I'm just fine right here...

1.4 Three Things I Love...

Music plays. The actors all come on together and talk right to us...

BABS. This scene is called: Three things I love.

   Beat.

I think you'll figure it out.

VANYA. Bad ice cream. Like really cheap ice cream sandwiches and those crappy cones wrapped in paper with chocolate and nuts on top—like...

SONIA. Drumsticks...?

VANYA. Drumsticks or or or...Nutty Buddys. Just really great, really bad ice cream.

ELLA. Old barns; ancient churches; abandoned buildings; all the old, empty, quiet, and sacred spaces of the world...

PROFESSOR. An elegant string quartet weaving impossibly sublime music out of midair...

BABS. The crisp clink of cubes of ice in a really *sturdy* glass...and what follows...

SONIA. Kindness. Tiny, meaningless, random acts of kindness.

ASTER. Putting my ears under the bathwater...that empty, muffled, drowning sound when you're the only creature on the planet for a hot, damp moment...

ELLA. Yes... I love that, too...

PICKLES. *(Still pulling herself together...)* Berry cobbler...

VANYA. A cool, cool pillow on a hot, hot night.

BABS. Dirt boys in boots who played the drums... God, I loved to nibble on those.

PROFESSOR. Her fingertips just softly brushing my arm or face, just...casually...lovingly...but in a way where everyone else in the room knows she is...*mine.*

PICKLES. *Nina Simone.* I mean...just the idea of *Nina Simone,* right?

BABS. Right…

SONIA. Kittens. *(Off of the reaction.)* I know, I know, but seriously… *kittens.*

ELLA. Tiny, dangerous boats.

VANYA. The really stupid jokes kids love. Like "Where does a general keep his armies?" "In his sleevies." Or "What did one wall say to the other? I'll meet you at the corner!" Those kinds of jokes…

ASTER. Really big, really ancient, really amazing Trees.

PICKLES. That face people make when they're really listening and want you to keep talking…not because they have something to say and they want you to finish, but when they truly want to hear what you have to say.

ELLA. That mysterious, unnamable moment when an orgasm becomes inevitable…

>*All the actors stop breathing for a long moment…*

PROFESSOR. Being right. Winning. And genuine approbation.

>*Tiny beat.*

Look it up.

SONIA. Fairy tales.

BABS. Adventures.

ASTOR. Ocelots.

1.5 Dance Card

>*They all look at him… Music. Folks move away, leaving Sonia and the Professor, who makes an effort to have a conversation…*

PROFESSOR. Ummm…Sonia?

SONIA. Yes?

PROFESSOR. *(Pulling this out of his ass a bit…)* You're…looking quite lovely today.

SONIA. Really?

PROFESSOR. Certainly. Did you…*cut your hair off*?

SONIA. Yes. Just a little over two years ago.

PROFESSOR. Ah. Well…

SONIA. How are you feeling? Any better?

PROFESSOR. Marginally. I'm afraid my case is terminal

SONIA. …what?!

PROFESSOR. Yes, it seems I'm suffering from something called O.L.D.

SONIA. Oh, my God, what's—oh. Ha ha.

PROFESSOR. Don't worry about me. I'm fine.

SONIA. Okay. I won't…

> Beat…

PROFESSOR. Well, I…I'll see you in a bit. I have some reading to do.

SONIA. Okay…

> *He kisses her on the forehead or the top of her head or some other kind of awkward semi-intimate gesture…then leaves. Sonia steps up to talk to us.*

So, do you know who all these people are? I was afraid it might be a bit confusing so I thought maybe I could give you a kind of… guide…or dance card… So, I'm Sonia, and this is my house—

> *She looks at the set…*

Well, an odd, impressionistic, deconstructed version of my house, anyway… I live here with my Uncle Vanya, my mother's little brother, and Babs, who's my aunt. Well, not my *actual* aunt, but my mother's best friend from college. Oh, my mom died when I was eleven. Breast cancer… And Babs came to live with us when my mom got sick, and then just…*stayed.* Thank God… Her real name is Bathsheba, but no one calls her that. She's a potter. No, no, a "Ceramic Artist." She made this!

> *The mug she has…*

She actually does pretty well, I guess, because she travels a lot now, sometimes for months at a time. Just disappears. "Off on an adventure..." she says, and she's gone.

So Vanya and Babs are my...*extended family*, I guess. Oh, and Pickles! Geez! I forgot her, but she lives here, too. She's...ummm... Vanya's step-half-sister...or half-step-sister...once removed...or something. So she's actually kind of my aunt, too, but she's not so much an aunt as she is—well, she's just Pickles. She's kind of an acquired taste. She lives in the apartment over the garage and she works at a group home for people with, you know, *challenges*. And she makes crafty things. She made this!

> *Holds up a thing.*

I'm can't say with any real authority, but she might just be the kindest, most loyal, biggest-hearted person on the entire planet... I'm just sayin'...

Dr. Aster is Uncle Vanya's oldest friend. They grew up together and he lives less than a mile away. Nine hundred and fifty-one steps, actually. More or less. Anyway... Sometimes he's here a lot, sometimes not. Just now, he is. Pretty much constantly, actually, for the last...seventy-two hours or so...

The one Vanya calls The Professor—that's my father. "Dear Old Dad." He left when I was seven. Before my mom got sick, but still... He and his third wife, Ella, have been here for a few days now. My mother was his first wife...

I guess they're kind of visiting. He tends to show up maybe once a year or so. Which is fine. He can be a lot of fun, actually. Or used to be. But this time around it all feels a little tense. *Family*, right? It's like everyone is hard-wired to totally upset everyone else.

> *Pickles enters and listens...*

Like, at breakfast yesterday I started imagining everyone had these buttons on their backs...like on an old blender, those solid push-buttons. Blend, Whip, Spindle, Mutilate, whatever. But these were like... Annoy... Provoke... Poke-At-Painful-Old-Wound. Things like that. *(Leaning in...)* The thing is—

1.6 Repudiate

PICKLES. Do you think love lasts forever?

SONIA. I'm sorry...?

PICKLES. Do you think love is *real*? A force. A real, actual, substantial thing in the world...like a rock...or selfishness...or do you think it's just an artificial man-made construct like religion...or football?

SONIA. Oh, man, *really*?

PICKLES. Yes, really. I'm just diggin' here, you know? Just diggin' around...

SONIA. I think it's real. Like a rock. (*Discovering this idea more fully as she goes...*) Exactly like rock, actually. Solid...weighty... hard...and painful in a variety of awful and humiliating ways...

PICKLES. That's what I think!

SONIA. Well, okay then...

PICKLES. (*Abruptly.*) Did you know that this play is called LIFE SUCKS?

SONIA. (*This is getting awkward...*) Ummm...yes.

PICKLES. Do you think that's right?

SONIA. Oh Pickles...

PICKLES. Do you think life sucks? Do you think that that's... *accurate*?

SONIA. Pickles we're not even at the end of Act One

PICKLES. 'Cause I don't. (*Including us...*) I don't think that title is right and I just want you to know that I didn't choose it...and furthermore, that I *repudiate it.*

SONIA. But—

PICKLES. That sounds funny. Repudiate. Repudiate. Repudiate. Repudiate. *Repudiate. Repudiate. Repudiate.* Is that even a word?

SONIA. Yes.

PICKLES. Does it mean...to deny. To reverse. To...erase?

SONIA. I think so. (*To us.*) Does it?

Hopefully the audience answers positively...

PICKLES. Okay, good. Well, then, I *repudiate* that title. Sure, life is hard, life is tricky. And it can be really unfair and frustrating and, you know...*deeply problematic* sometimes. Right? Right?

SONIA. Right.

PICKLES. But life does not *suck*. I just wanted to get that on the record. Not that there's a record or whatever, I know that, but I wanted to get that on the record anyway. Life does not suck. *Life* does not *suck*. Life does *not* suck.

SONIA. End of Act One.

> *There is probably a song here as we transition from Act One to Act Two.*

End of Act One

ACT TWO: THE MUDDLE IN THE MIDDLE OF THE NIGHT

2.0 My Wife

Late that night the Professor and Babs are drinking. He's in some pain, maybe in his joints or his body overall. It is hard for him to get comfortable...

PROFESSOR. My wife. My third *wife*...

BABS. Yes...

PROFESSOR. This *fascinating*...this *captivating*...this insanely *alluring* creature...

BABS. ...yes?

PROFESSOR. *Hates me.*

BABS. Oh?

PROFESSOR. *And loves me...*

BABS. Of course...

PROFESSOR. I mean, she must love me a little, or she wouldn't have married me, right?

BABS. Absolutely.

PROFESSOR. But, no, beyond any question, she hates me now, too. As only a wife can... A kind of...*glacial...long-simmering... cat-footed* little hatred... a glowing-embers-long-into-the-night kind of hatred.

BABS. Gosh...

PROFESSOR. I don't know what she was thinking. I mean, look at me...

BABS. Ummm...

PROFESSOR. No, seriously, look at me. This is what I look like. Exactly this. This is *me.*

BABS. Yes it is.

PROFESSOR. And, if you'll recall, I didn't look much better when we met, in case you were wondering…or *excusing*…or judging…

BABS. I wasn't…

PROFESSOR. No, maybe not. Maybe that's why I can talk to you. You don't judge, do you?

BABS. Not much, no.

PROFESSOR. Why is that?

BABS. Oh…

PROFESSOR. No, seriously, why?

BABS. Oh, my twenties, I guess. After a certain quantity of unnecessarily stupid choices and thoughtless acts—some with real consequences—I decided one probably ought to relinquish the right to judge others for anything…

PROFESSOR. I see.

> *Quick beat.*

Were these…indiscretions of—?

BABS. Oh shhhh. No stories. Besides, you're asking for the wrong reasons. Anyway, you were saying? About you and your wife and how you look…?

PROFESSOR. Oh. Oh, yes… Well, here's the thing. Here's the odd little lacuna of my life…

BABS. Lacuna?

PROFESSOR. Umm…unfilled, unknown space. Puzzle. Gap…

BABS. Gotchya.

PROFESSOR. Ready?

BABS. Astound me.

PROFESSOR. I don't look like this in my mind.

BABS. No?

PROFESSOR. Not even close.

BABS. Really?

PROFESSOR. Absolutely.

BABS. So…what do you look like in your mind?

PROFESSOR. Better. Much better. My self-image is…amazingly better than the reality.

Even as I speak to you, at this precise moment, when I picture in my mind what you're looking at, though I know for a fact that you are seeing…*this (Gestures to himself.)* …what I imagine is something much closer to… *oh, Sean Connery circa *The Untouchables*, maybe…or Alan Rickman in *Sense and Sensibility*…rather than…a slightly bloated, badly aging Bill Maher.*

Whereas—and here is the oddest part of my much-maligned married life—I'm afraid my wife's self-image works unrelentingly in the opposite direction.

BABS. Really?

PROFESSOR. Absolutely. Shockingly, her self-image leads her to perceive herself much less like the near-*Cate Blanchett*-like siren that she really is, and more like a… sweaty, disheveled *Lena Dunham* after a 10K charity run for Africa…

BABS. You are such—

PROFESSOR. *(Ignoring her, going on…)* And what I think happened here is…well, I think her self-image somehow fell in love, ass over teacup, with my self-image. So when people see us together they tend to think "What the fuck?"—which I have to tell you is not a great deal of fun when you see it play so rampantly across the faces of people you are being introduced to for the first time over and over and over again. But…if they could see us as we so oddly see *ourselves*…then they'd probably think: "Hmm. Seems about right."

BABS. Well, that's…that's quite a—

2.1 Change!

Ella enters, sees him…

ELLA. Oh, hey… You're still awake? Hi Babs.

BABS. Hi. *(Getting up right away…)* And bye…

ELLA. You don't have to go.

33

BABS. Oh, yes I do. It's late. Nighty-night you two lovebirds. See you in the morn.

ELLA. Good night.

Babs leaves slightly awkwardly...

What were you two / talking

PROFESSOR. Nothing.

ELLA. Oh, God, were you really talking about us?

PROFESSOR. No, no, I was just

ELLA. Robert...

PROFESSOR. I just can't—I can't quite believe that it's come to *this*. It's like everything I touch eventually turns to shit, I / can't catch

ELLA. Well, that's awfully sweet of you...

PROFESSOR. a break, and I end up feeling horrible most of the time, trapped in an insupportable, perdurable miasma / of lost

ELLA. Oh, please just *talk*! Don't...*write it*! Just say it!

PROFESSOR. This is me! This is how I talk. This is who / I am!

ELLA. Then change! Try to change for the better! For me!

PROFESSOR. You change! *You try!* Try—you know—*LIKING ME*, for instance!

ELLA. Oh, Lord Almighty, not again, I love you, you fucking idiot, but that doesn't mean you automatically get a free pass on / every annoying

PROFESSOR. So you don't like the way I *talk*? You really want me to change how I *talk*?!?

ELLA. Yes! I *do*. I really do. You don't talk *to* people anymore, you talk *at* them, or or or through them, or...or *over* their heads in order to humiliate them.

PROFESSOR. Oh, please...!

ELLA. *(Going right on...)* What was that with Vanya today, with the Virgil quote?

PROFESSOR. That? That was a perfectly apropos reference / that was appropriate

ELLA. Oh please! You did it to shame him. You rubbed your Virgil

34

in his face like an old dead fish! You've gotten meaner, you have.

PROFESSOR. That's a stupid thing to say.

ELLA. It's not! When did you become such a flagrant prick? You weren't always this way, were you? Or were you, and I just couldn't see it?

PROFESSOR. *(Truly taken aback…)* I have no idea how to answer a question that asinine.

ELLA. There's contempt in your voice, Robert, and that can't be a good thing! Vanya can be as annoying as it gets, but he's not an idiot and he's not the devil, and we're trying to make nice here, / not piss everyone off.

PROFESSOR. *(Agreeing sheepishly, perhaps…)* I know, I know, you're right, you're right…

ELLA. And I'm sorry if your whole life has "gone to shit," but I'm still part of that life / and I'd appreciate it

PROFESSOR. That's not what I meant…!

ELLA. if you'd pull your head out of your ass and make a fucking effort!

PROFESSOR. Oh, God, I don't feel well.

ELLA. *(Having tread this path before…)* No, no of course not…

PROFESSOR. It's not my fault. I'm all achy…

ELLA. Did you have dinner?

PROFESSOR. No. I couldn't bear the idea…

ELLA. Oh, great, now I get the Trifecta: Sick, tired, *and* hungry. Now you'll be cruel on top / of being cranky and pouty

PROFESSOR. Oh, I'm so sorry if my pain is inconvenient to you!

ELLA. so you'll be *completely* unbearable.

PROFESSOR. I thought I was *already* completely / unbearable. Aren't you—

ELLA. *More* unbearable, *extra, super-duper* unbearable why in God's name would you choose *that* to pick a fight about / in the wee hours…

PROFESSOR. Go to bed, then, go / to bed.…

ELLA. *You* go to bed! *You* go!

35

PROFESSOR. Oh, so you can go chat with Vanya! Or / the doctor! Or

ELLA. Oh, please, you are so pathetic!

PROFESSOR. I am, I am pathetic, I love you / so much, and I know you

ELLA. Oh, God, no, not that, please anything but that small, clingy, ingratiating horseshit, do you want to drive me / away forever…?

PROFESSOR. I know, I know, I'm sorry, / I just

ELLA. You're so infuriating! I'm going for a walk! / Goodnight!

PROFESSOR. Wait, come back, I—

She is gone.

2.2 Gray Nose Hairs

PROFESSOR. *(Abruptly to us…)* Well, that didn't go well.

You know what I hate worst about aging? About turning into an old man…?

You get a little pain. A little…*condition*. Some insignificant nothing, but it hurts, so now you can't exercise, so you gain a little weight, and that's depressing, so you drink a little more scotch, or eat a little more ice cream or indulge whatever your particular predilection may be to stave off the encroaching depression, and the awful cycle has begun… more pain, more weight, more indulgence, more depression, pain, weight, indulgence, depression, and on and on and on and…

Same thing psychologically, right? One day you just feel kind of *old*. Or *wrinkled*. So you get a little low, a little insecure. Which is less attractive. And she sees you're insecure. So you get *more* insecure. So you retreat. So she retreats. Or *attacks*. So you attack. Or overcompensate. And she fucking hates that. And so on and so on till *death*…or *divorce*…or *disdain*…or the most common of all the awful Ds…*disengagement*.

And then there you are. The rest of your life. And it sucks. All because of a gouty knee. Or gray nose hairs. Or any of the thousand and one tiny indignities of the irreparably aging human body. It isn't fair. And it isn't kind.

It is, however, sadly inevitable.

But the thing is…the key thing you have to understand about life is this:

Beat. Beat...

Oh, fuck it, I'm too tired. I'm gonna take some pills and see what dreams may come to visit this decaying mortal coil... Nighty-night.

2.3 Pre-Abstract

Scene shifts. Ella and Vanya enter, mid-conversation. He is more following Ella than walking with her. She is agitated and frustrated. It is late...

ELLA. Why aren't you asleep?

VANYA. Why aren't you?

ELLA. I wish I were.

VANYA. I wish I were pre-abstract.

ELLA. What? I mean—what???

VANYA. That's what I wish. I wish I lived before the dawn of abstraction.

ELLA. *(Puzzling through a quick beat before...)* What does that even *mean*?

VANYA. Imagine The Garden, before...you know, before the snake fucked the goose and we all got kicked out on our metaphorical asses.

ELLA. Are you drunk?

VANYA. Some.

ELLA. Oh, God...

VANYA. Doesn't that sound wonderful? To be pre-abstract. Think about it!

ELLA. Is this another of your ridiculous—because I have a pedicure a year from Thursday, so I might not have / time to fully...

VANYA. I'm just saying: The Apple is *Abstraction*.

ELLA. Which apple?

VANYA. THE Apple. Eve's apple. What other apple—?

ELLA. Ah, Eve.

VANYA. I mean—knowledge of Good and Evil? Please, what does that even mean? But the dawn of the capacity for abstract thought…? Okay, imagine you've spent your entire existence living in the present—in the *moment*—in the perpetual, instinctual NOW of the animal kingdom…

ELLA. Okay.

VANYA. …and then suddenly, somehow, Boom! Abstract thought! Just like that! (Like when my father used to wake me up for a trip he would walk into my room, four A.M., turn on the light, tear the comforter off the bed, and yell "get up!"

ELLA. Jesus…

VANYA. Yeah, I know, but effective! Welcome to the fucking world! Good luck!) So I imagine the Dawn of Abstraction like that. There you are in your pre-dawn REM sleep, dreaming of simple things like muffins and blow jobs and then… Shwannk!!!!! Good Morning Death and Complexity! Somehow we woke up to Abstraction and there we were—hurled unwittingly into the impossible early-morning light of existence by our own ridiculous brains! You see what I'm saying…?

ELLA. I understand the idea, but I don't / know what

VANYA. Because the truth is… I don't really want to know that I'm going to die! Why would I want that? Why would anyone??? I don't want to be able to to to to *extrapolate* possible futures or ruminate on the ridiculous choices of my past or or or be bound by man-made constructs like morality or fidelity or… *I fantasize about a life before we knew how to fantasize…*

ELLA. *(A positive, thoughtful response, finally…)* Hmm…that's…

VANYA. I wish to God (in whom I emphatically do not believe…) that I could just live blissfully in the present—The Ridiculous Present—of wanting to eat that delicious thing…or make love to that beautiful woman…or sleep in that shady spot and just…you know…be content. Just…*content.*

ELLA. *(With real warmth for the first time.)* I must say…content does sound nice…

VANYA. Run away with me.

ELLA. Oh my God!

VANYA. Walk out the door with me and never look back.

ELLA. What are you doing?

VANYA. Living in the Ridiculous Present!

ELLA. You ruin everything, you know that? You're like Shiva…

VANYA. Isn't that a restaurant?

ELLA. It's the Hindu God of Destruction.

VANYA. I knew that.

ELLA. You're like a terrible little six-year-old on the playground. "I want that!" "Mine!" "Mine Mine Mine!" And if you can't have it—if some other little devil already has it—you throw a tantrum.

VANYA. So I'm like a six-year-old God of Destruction, is that right? A Child Shiva? Is that the story you want to tell yourself to protect yourself from the truth?

ELLA. What truth?

VANYA. That I'm your *bashert*. I'm the other part of your soul. I could not feel what I feel for you if we were not connected somehow. If there weren't something important and…*true*…between us. You must feel that…

ELLA. I don't.

VANYA. You must.

ELLA. You're an idiot.

VANYA. That's immaterial.

She starts to go, maybe kind of laughing…

ELLA. I don't believe you…!

VANYA. Believe me! Trust me. Love me…!

ELLA. Shut up! Would you please just shut up, leave me alone, and learn to live in this broken, ridiculous, *post*-abstract world. Life is hard. Love is hard. Days are long and hard, and death, like it or not, is coming for all of us the day after tomorrow, more or less. Now pull yourself together, get your tongue off the floor, stop acting like a lovesick poodle, and do something useful for SOMEONE ELSE, for God's sake. Be a Person! How's that for *bashert*?!?

She storms away. He waits a beat. Looks at us.

VANYA. Isn't she wonderful? You see it, right? She has a big soul. I would die for her. Do you think she likes me, deep down? Do you think I have a chance? Seriously. I'm asking. Seriously...

> *They answer. Or don't. If they do, maybe there is a real discussion about Unrequited Love or Mismatched Love or Unbalanced love or... After the conversation has run its course, he yells to the wings...*

Next!

2.4 Lost & Drunk

Aster stumbles on and falls down somehow, ripping his pants...

ASTER. Ouch!!! Fuck A Duck on a Doily!

SONIA. What's going on? Are you okay?

ASTER. Ella?

SONIA. *(Appearing.)* No. It's me, Sonia.

ASTER. Oh. Hey kid.

SONIA. Sorry to disappoint you.

ASTER. I'm not disappointed, I'm wounded. Though I think it's just my ass and my dignity.

> *He feels his ass and finds a rip in his pants.*

Oh. And my pants...

SONIA. What were you doing?

ASTER. Drinking, mostly.

SONIA. No, how did you rip your pants?

ASTER. Falling down, waddaya think? Drinking and falling down go together, like cheese & crackers...or Laurel & Hardy...or Marx & Engels...

SONIA. *(Referring to his pants.)* Let me see them.

ASTER. You can't. Marx & Engels have been dead for years.

SONIA. No, your pants.

ASTER. Oh. Why didn't you say so. Look!

He shows her the big rip in his pants...

SONIA. Wow.

ASTER. Yeah.

SONIA. Take 'em off.

ASTER. I'm sorry?

SONIA. Take off your pants.

ASTER. *(Southern?)* Why, Sonia, I'm not that kind of boy...!

SONIA. Just take them off. I can fix them in five minutes.

ASTER. Okay, thanks. Wait...

He looks down his pants to see what he's wearing under them.

Okay, I think we should be safe.

He takes his pants off...

SONIA. Why do you drink so much?

ASTER. Why do you drink so little?

SONIA. I'm *serious.*

ASTER. Oh, you're "serious." Well, then...

SONIA. Why? Is it because you're sad?

ASTER. Sad? *Moi?*

SONIA. *Seriously!*

ASTER. *(Suddenly.)* Of course I'm sad! How can you not be sad these days? Have you seen the world? Has the...pony express not sent dispatches from the front?

SONIA. Ummm...

ASTER. The world is going to hand in a hellbasket!

SONIA. I don't think that's / a thing.

ASTER. Fucking Sad or Fucking Mad are about the only real options left these days for anyone sane, and mad takes too much energy, and I need what's left of my energy for drinking, so I tend to choose sad...

SONIA. You never take me seriously.

ASTER. Okay... Okay. I'm ready... I am about to take you seriously.

41

Sobering or straightening himself up... Maybe slaps himself a few times...

Okay. Okay, I'm ready.

Beat.

Ummm...what did you want to know again?

SONIA. Why are you sad? Why do you drink so much? You could be so... What's the matter with you? That's what I want to know. What's *wrong*?

ASTER. Wow. Okay... Well, kid, I guess the truth is I just can't—I can't quite seem to...*care*, I guess. I just find it kind of hard to...you know...*care*. About anything.

SONIA. But you seem to care about *everything*.

ASTER. *(Bottom line.)* And *that's* why I'm sad.

Beat. Beat...

SONIA. I have a friend...

ASTER. Oh?

SONIA. And she's...well, a little obsessed, I'm afraid, with a man maybe a bit like you. Successful...handsome, charming...slightly eccentric, maybe, but with many positive virtues. But older and still unsettled. And drinks, too, like you.

ASTER. *(Joking-ish...)* You're not just talking about me, are you?

SONIA. No! No, not at all. That would be creepy.

ASTER. Oh, okay. Sorry... Go on...

SONIA. Anyway... This *man* doesn't seem to notice her...you know...as a *woman*.

ASTER. I see. And...?

SONIA. What should she do? I don't think she wants to love him, but I don't think she can help it. I don't want to overstate it, but it's kind of...you know...

ASTER. What?

SONIA. Ruining her life. It's kind of ruining her life.

ASTER. Is she pretty?

SONIA. No.

ASTER. Oh. Not at all?

SONIA. Not so much.

> *Quick beat.*

(Small and dark...) Nice hair. Nice eyes...

ASTER. Too bad. Tell her to run away as fast as she can. He sounds like a fucking nightmare. If he's anything like me he's a perfect recipe for disaster. I'm a trap. You know what my second ex-fiancée called me?

SONIA. No.

ASTER. "A perfect lover in every way except all the most important ways."

SONIA. That sounds bad.

ASTER. 'Bout as bad as it gets. *(Pulling himself up...)* I should probably be / on—

SONIA. My mother used to say that our house was full of Radiant Invisible Butterflies.

ASTER. *(Taken aback...)* Oh?

SONIA. Yes. And every so often she'd call a Hunt and a wild family excursion for Radiant Invisible Butterflies (or R.I.B.s) would be on. I was really young, but I remember these episodes quite clearly. They were high points. But when I got older—I don't know, maybe seven or eight, I finally asked her The Question. The Big One: Were they *real*? Were there *really* Radiant Invisible Butterflies fluttering around our house? Were there *really*?

ASTER. And what did she tell you?

SONIA. She told me they were just as real as I wanted them to be. She told me that the world was what *we made of it*. She told me that we had cause and effect all wrong, that we thought the world did things to us, and that *that* was the cause of our joy or suffering or *sadness* or whatever... But she said that that was totally wrong. *She said we were the cause.* She said we *choose* to be joyful or to suffer or to be sad...*and that we could always choose differently. That anything was possible.* If we could imagine...new possibilities.

> *Beat...*

ASTER. Listen: Tell your friend... Run Away. *Fast.* Good night.

He starts off. He comes back…

Umm…can I have my pants?

SONIA. They're not done.

ASTER. Okay. I can walk home in this. Maybe old Mrs. Farfennugen / will call the sheriff on me and we can cause a scandal.

SONIA. *(Gently correcting him…)* Farnsworth.

ASTER. G'night, kid. Sweet dreams…

He leaves.

SONIA. Oh. My. God. "I have a friend"? And butterflies? "Invisible *butterflies*"?
Where did that even come from?!?
I just told him some insane story about Radiant Invisible Butterflies when all I wanted to say was "Please, please, please, take me upstairs right now, tear my stupid clothes off my stupid body with your teeth and fucking fuck me so hard and so well and so long that that that…that the bed breaks, and the universe disappears, and the sun stops in its rotation to see what all the fuss is about and the world comes crashing to a stop and our epic, ridiculous, sublime love-making is the last thing that the universe ever knows."
But instead…I made up some story about invisible butterflies in a pathetic attempt to let him know I understand him and that he could do with me as he would…and I could see, totally clearly in his face that *he didn't get the message.* Not even close. It never even occurred to him because he cannot see me as a woman. Because the women that are real to him aren't like me…

Ella enters upstage somewhere…

They're a lot more like her…

2.5 Oh. Hello

ELLA. Oh. Hello.

SONIA. *(Gently mocking…)* Oh. Hello.

ELLA. Am I interrupting?

SONIA. No. I mean—no.

ELLA. Are you all right?

SONIA. Of course.

ELLA. Really?

SONIA. No. I mean…yes, of course.

ELLA. You seem

SONIA. What?

ELLA. I don't know. Do you want to…talk to me about it? I would so like us to be friends but I can't help but feel

SONIA. Yes…?

ELLA. that you sort of

SONIA. What?

ELLA. Hate me. I can't help but feel you sort of hate me.

SONIA. I do! I do hate you, I hate you so much I can barely stand to look at you. Except that I'm just a little bit in love with you, too… Or *infatuated*…or *bewitched* like everyone else, and of course I envy you absurdly and I want to to to slap you hard right across the face but then also bring you a rum and Coke and talk with you on the carpet with our shoes off until four A.M. and tell you all about everything / that is—

ELLA. Great! Let's start with the slap.

SONIA. What?

ELLA. Let's start with the slap. I understand you perfectly and I'm thrilled you're finally talking to me and I think the only thing for it is that we do just as you suggest but I don't think any of it can happen without the slap, so…ready?

SONIA. You're my stepmother. I'm not going / to just slap

ELLA. I am not leaving this room until you slap me hard, just once, right across / the face.

SONIA. Are you crazy? Why would I slap you?

ELLA. Let's not waste time, I want the rum and Coke and the girl-talk so—!

> Sonia slaps her once, HARD, right across the face. She is immediately astounded at what she has done…

45

SONIA. Oh my God!

ELLA. *(Surprised more than hurt, but still…)* That hurt!

SONIA. Oh God! I'm so, so sorry!

ELLA. That hurt!

SONIA. Are you okay?

ELLA. No, I'm not okay! You just slapped me across the damn face!

SONIA. I know! I did! I really did!

ELLA. How did it feel?

SONIA. Great!

ELLA. Good.

SONIA. How did it feel to you?

ELLA. It hurt! It's still stinging. Now go!

SONIA. Go?

ELLA. Go get me a rum and Coke! And get one for yourself, too.

SONIA. Okay.

ELLA. And then I want to hear all about it.

SONIA. Ummm…

ELLA. Go.

SONIA. Okay. I…ummm…okay!

> *She goes.*

ELLA. *(To us.)* I like her. I think she's a good person. She's like…an avocado. You know? Kind of good and good for you and with a kind of weird texture… I don't know what made me think that. I've never compared anyone to a fruit—or vegetable—before. *(To the audience.)* Is an avocado a fruit or a vegetable?

> *She hopefully gets an answer…*

Good. Thanks. Anyway, I'd like to be her friend. I'd like to help her… I think that would feel good.

2.6 Friends

SONIA. *(Returning hastily...)* Okay, here, I just brought the mixings... the Coke...and the rum, of course... And some snacks.

ELLA. Perfect.

SONIA. Yeah?

ELLA. Sure. Though I don't actually love rum and Coke, it was more a...metaphor. A metaphorical drink rather than—

SONIA. Do you want something else?

ELLA. No. This is fine... The play will bog down if / you...

SONIA. Okay.

ELLA. Okay. So.

SONIA. Yes...?

ELLA. What's wrong?

SONIA. With?

ELLA. No. *(Making it larger...)* What's *wrong*?

SONIA. You mean with everything?

ELLA. What...in *particular*.

SONIA. Well, you know... *Love*, I guess.

ELLA. Ah. Specifically, or in general.

SONIA. Specifically.

ELLA. The doctor?

SONIA. How did you know?

ELLA. Are you serious? Everyone knows.

SONIA. I don't care. I'm not ashamed of my love. I love him so much, and I think I could make him happy. I think I could be exactly what he needs / if he

ELLA. Oh, dear...

SONIA. What?

ELLA. Nothing.

SONIA. What? I know what love is. I do. Just because I don't look like *you* doesn't mean / I don't

47

ELLA. Whoa there…

SONIA. What?

ELLA. Who said you have to look / like anything to understand

SONIA. I get it. I know what I look like. Everyone thinks that if you look like me you have to settle for, you know… All The Steve Buscemis Of The World, but—

ELLA. You are lovely.

SONIA. No I'm not.

ELLA. You are.

SONIA. No I'm not.

ELLA. Sonia, you have / beautiful

SONIA. Stop! I swear to God if you say *eyes* or *hair* I will cut your heart out with this swizzle stick!

ELLA. Oh.

SONIA. We all know the codes. You know your code, what the glances and looks and little touches you get mean…you know *sexy lady code*, right?

ELLA. Umm…

SONIA. Right?!

ELLA. Yes, I guess so…

SONIA. Well I know *ugly girl code*. I know / what the looks

ELLA. You're not—

SONIA. Whatever. Homely. Plain. Nice-looking. "Lovely." "A great person." "She's just terrific." "What a great personality." And the worst one, the most brutal code there is—Nice *eyes*. Nice *hair*.

ELLA. Okay. Okay, so… You're not that pretty. Is that what you want to hear?

SONIA. Yes! It is. Thank you.

ELLA. You actually *do* have…some lovely physical qualities…but I get that they don't quite add up to the picture you might want them to. How's that?

SONIA. Good. Now you're being a good stepmother. You're telling me the *truth*.

ELLA. Well good. I so want us to be…friends.

SONIA. Then keep being honest with me.

ELLA. I will. And you be honest with me.

SONIA. I will.

ELLA. So about the doctor…

SONIA. Oh, God.

ELLA. Tell me about it. Does he know how you feel?

SONIA. No! I mean… I don't think so. I haven't, you know…

ELLA. Told him. Or shown him.

SONIA. Shown?

ELLA. You know…lingering glances. Casual touches. "I like you" code…

SONIA. No. Never.

ELLA. Never?

SONIA. Well…I just told him a story about butterflies, but it was a disaster.

ELLA. Ummm…

SONIA. What's the point? He loves women like *you*. And they love him. So what hope do I have? Even though I know I could be better for him than anyone else in the world. I could save him. I could give him everything he needs if he could just see past my stupid face and…whatever…and just…love me.

ELLA. What about what *you* need?

SONIA. I don't need anything! I have *too many* things! I want to give my things away. I'm out of room inside. I'm like an emotional hoarder. I have to give some of my heart to someone or I'm going to explode!

ELLA. Sonia, you have *no idea what you're talking about*. You can't just give and give and give even if it feels like you could. You're just *wrong*. And if you try to give give give to those that are willing to take take take…well, it usually doesn't end up so well. In fact, it *never* ends up well.

SONIA. Well, thanks. You've cheered me up tremendously.

ELLA. Now hold on…

SONIA. What, I'm just wrong and stupid and young and ugly and you're gonna be my friend by just pointing out how wrong / I am about *everything*.

ELLA. I'm trying my best to be helpful, to help / you see that you're not looking at this with the clearest eyes so you can

SONIA. Wait, here, take my swizzle stick so you can poke me in the eye, too!

ELLA. I'm trying to be / your friend and

SONIA. Shut up! Don't try to help me by telling me I'm bad and wrong!!! Being honest doesn't mean you have to be a condescending bitch!
Oh, God, I'm sorry. I'm just so, so, so unhappy.
You can't make someone love you, can you?

ELLA. Well…

SONIA. Or maybe *you* can, but *I* can't. *I can't.* I'm just me. I'm just nothing but…*me*. I hate that so much.

ELLA. I'm so sorry you do.

SONIA. Life sucks.

ELLA. No it doesn't.

SONIA. Life *sucks*.

ELLA. No. It doesn't.

SONIA. Oh. Well… What does life do, then?

>*Ella searches for an answer…*

ELLA. Uh… It… Ummm…
(To audience.) Intermission.

>*Blackout.*

End of Act Two

ACT THREE: NEEDS

3.0 Incomprehensible

Aster and Ella are together, maybe eating or drinking, but they have been talking for some time, just the two of them… Ella is intrigued and amused by him. Aster is utterly enthralled by her every everything… He is thinking about her as much or more than what he is saying…

ASTER. It's practically incomprehensible.

ELLA. Is it?

ASTER. And will, I think, become only more so as the future horribly unfolds…

ELLA. Ah…

ASTER. They'll undoubtedly condemn us. The People of the Future—if they somehow muddle through and there ARE People of the Future—will look back at our incomprehensible choices and policies and boundless selfishness and think: Just what—by all that is Holy—could they possibly have been thinking?!?! Is greed THAT powerful?

Or did they somehow think you could have…you know…an apple tree, say, a single lovely Apple Tree and just, you know, pick a bunch of apples…and then pick a bunch more…and then pick a quarter of the apples one day, and then another quarter, and then another quarter, and then another quarter and then another quarter and another quarter and another quarter and another quarter and that this could go on FOR EVER?

You see what I'm saying?

ELLA. Yeah, I get it, of course, / I do, but…

ASTER. Or maybe…maybe they'll believe we thought the Earth was so big we couldn't get our minds around the fact that we were systematically destroying it. Maybe they'll believe that the Earth

51

seemed SO big and SO strong and so *indestructible* that we thought it really *was* indestructible and therefore that we could do whatever we pleased with total impunity…

But I don't think they'll think that.

ELLA. No?

ASTER. No. I think they'll just hate us.

ELLA. Yes, I expect so…

ASTER. The list is already incomprehensible and it's growing every day. Rampant extinctions. Ravaged ecosystems. Raping the earth. Polluting the seas. Decimating the forests. Mutating the crops. What are we thinking…?

ELLA. I don't know…

ASTER. You are unbelievably bored by me, aren't you?

ELLA. No, no, not by *you*…

ASTER. Oh?

ELLA. Just by what you're *saying.*

ASTER. Ah…

ELLA. I think *you* are wonderfully interesting much of the time. Though why you are so…

ASTER. …obsessed?

ELLA. Exactly…is beyond me. Even if everything you say is true. Which I'm sure it is. Even if we are ravishing the world and destroying the glaciers and the rainforests and the horny owls and / lizards and

ASTER. Spotted owls…

ELLA. whatever, and ruining everything, even if that's ALL true… what are we supposed to do about it? Seriously? Seriously, I want to know.

> *During this Ella dials her cell, either real or fake…*

ASTER. Um…

ELLA. "Excuse me, *Mr. Tillerson*?" *(To Aster.)* CEO of Exxon… *(On phone.)* "Could you please…stop drilling? We think it's very bad. For the *world.* What's that? Oh, you *will*? Really? Gosh, thanks, that would be lovely…"

ASTER. I know it / won't be

ELLA. The die is cast. You know? It's *cast*. We went *this* direction. Don't you think? Big choices were made hundreds of years ago and now…well, there are huge, complex, well-funded, historical and financial forces that were put in motion generations ago, and…well…you can't go backwards, can you?

The world can't go backwards. The government can't go backwards. Exxon can't go backwards. I can't go backwards. Nothing can go backwards. *Nothing ever goes backwards.* Everything just has to do what it has to do…

ASTER. Would you…

ELLA. What?

ASTER. …want to go backwards?

ELLA. I'm sorry?

ASTER. You put *you* on the list. You said the world, the government, *you*… Would you want to go backwards? *(With significance…)* Do things differently?

ELLA. I just meant…

ASTER. I think I know what you meant. And I think you know what I mean. Don't you?

ELLA. I think so…

ASTER. So? If everything just…*has to do what it has to do*…

ELLA. Please don't. I don't think I can take it…

ASTER. You know what's going on here. You're feeling the same things I'm feeling, I know you are. Am I wrong? Am I completely delusional?

ELLA. No, no, / but I…

> *During this, Vanya, a bouquet of flowers in hand, appears and sees them. He hides and listens to the rest of this, amazed and appalled…*

ASTER. What's happening here is real. It's *real*.

ELLA. No, it's / not.

ASTER. It is! I have no idea what it is or what it means, but this is the world, this is *life*, this is LIFE, and all I know is I want you so badly I can hardly form a coherent thought or finish / a fucking sentence…

ELLA. *(To us and herself and the universe...)* I can't believe this is my life!

ASTER. Will you meet me later?

ELLA. No.

ASTER. No?

ELLA. No!

ASTER. Why not?

ELLA. *Because you're just another kind of backwards.*

ASTER. No, I'm not!

ELLA. Oh, trust me, you are! I've been where you want me to go and it is not a place I can live. I have to go forward no matter how I feel / about it, even if

ASTER. Why? Whose rule is that? Who says that that's the way it has / to be?

ELLA. I do...

ASTER. Well, I think you're wrong. I think you're an amazing creature / and I think

ELLA. Oh, God...

ASTER. we owe it to ourselves and to the universe to give whatever this is between us a chance and see where it might take us and what new paths in our lives might open up because of it.

> *She grabs him and kisses him hard on the mouth for several seconds, like a quick meal, and then just as abruptly, breaks away.*

So you'll meet me?

ELLA. No.

ASTER. But—

ELLA. You should go.

ASTER. You're—*incomprehensible.*

ELLA. Like the world? Like the apple tree?

ASTER. Precisely.

ELLA. Well, there you go then.

ASTER. Where?

ELLA. I have no idea. Now, please, leave me alone. For five fucking minutes. Please!

> *He gets up. Beat. He leaves… Vanya, in shock, leaves too… Ella turns abruptly to us and fills us in on where she is and how she is feeling…*

3.1 The Gavotte

ELLA. I like people, I really do. I find us all…*fascinating*. And *mysterious*. And kind of irresistibly fucked up in such unique and broken little ways. I genuinely want to know people and connect with them, I really do, but…

Can I ask you all a question?

How many of you would like to sleep with me if you could?

I mean, hypothetically, if there were no rules, no issues of *fidelity* or *morality*…or even *meta-theatricality*… Just based on whatever it is you know about me right at this moment, can we get a show of hands…?

How many of you would just…pretty much like to have sex with me?

> *She counts, and then maybe comments…or not…*

Okay, fascinating. And now another question…

How many of you are currently just dying to sleep with someone other than the person you should be sleeping with? Show of hands, please…

> *Again she counts, and then maybe comments…or not…*

Okay. Great.

Now… You don't have to raise your hands for this one, but…

How many of you were lying? Either because of who you are here with, or how you want to be thought of in the world, or because of my feelings, or…

Okay, here's my point: As far as I can tell, we're all just in a twisty, impossible, fucked up…yes, okay, *perdurable miasma* of "unmanageable urges" vs. "moral imperatives," and instead of being able to just…*connect*…just be in a kind and loving communion with our fellow human beings, we're forever wrapped up in this…sexual *dance macabre*…this *ridiculous relational gavotte*…this endless pursuit (and retreat) of *unexpressed, unfulfilled, unexplored, unknowable needs* and *desires* and *frustrations* and—

3.2 A Way

Vanya appears with manic, twisted energy. He is frantic and determined, now that he knows she is assailable, to win her for himself…

VANYA. Okay, look—

ELLA. Oh, no…

VANYA. *(Launching right in…)* So there has to be a *way*, right? A a a a

ELLA. Vanya…

VANYA. no no, hold on…a a a a a magic word…a gesture or or or *something* so compelling that you'll suddenly see me in a whole new light, and just *begin* to *imagine* that there's the merest possibility of you…*loving me back.*

ELLA. *(To audience.)* You see what I mean?

VANYA. There must be. Some…*avenue*? Some…amazingly persuasive argument…

ELLA. Argument?

VANYA. Or story? Or or or…*insight*? A view into the previously locked room of my soul that will touch some new place in you, put my finger on your button…

ELLA. …Vanya…

VANYA. …I mean… A *story* or or or anecdote that will make what at this moment seems…you know…the usual…*pathetic* and *repellant* and whatnot…suddenly seem *moving* and *endearing* and so wonderfully human that your icy heart will / melt and and and

ELLA. *(A tiny sarcastic toss-away…)* "Icy heart" is nice…

VANYA. you will see me as I am on the inside, and / begin to—

ELLA. And what is that?

VANYA. What?

ELLA. What is that? What are you like on the inside that is so different from what you are like on the outside?

VANYA. Uh…

ELLA. You've said / this over and

VANYA. It's not that—

ELLA. No wait, let me talk. You've said this over and over in all kinds of odd little ways. "The *real* me." "What I'm really like on the inside." "Who I *really* am." So fine, great, I'm ready, I'm all ears. And eyes. And…whatever: *What are you?* What is so fucking different about you on the inside…?

VANYA. Well, I can't just suddenly explain—

ELLA. Why not? Why the hell not?
I've listened to you talk and talk and whine and moan off and on for…a decade or so…and you know, I think I have a pretty good idea of who you are and how you operate and what you think and feel and want, and how you…present yourself in the world. By all the standard, accepted measures, I Know You. I know you pretty darn well.
Not *intimately*, maybe, but…pretty darn well.
So…I've rambled here. I've given you some time to gather your addled and surprised wits. So…enlighten me. What are you like inside?
What is going on in there that is SO different that you want me to know?

    A fairly protracted pause…

VANYA. Oh my God.
Nothing.
That's your answer.
Not a thing.
You're absolutely right. *This* is the "real me." This is it. This is all there is. This is me. And if I were you…I wouldn't be interested in me either.

ELLA. Vanya...

VANYA. I swear to God it all just hit me. Just *now*. For the first time...

I think my whole life I've been saying to myself—not just about you, but all the way back as far as this kind of thing goes. I've always thought "she" would choose me if only she really *knew me*. If she understood me. If only she knew what I'm really like, what I'm like deep down inside. How I mean so well. How much I want to do the right thing. How good my heart is.

How much I hurt. How confused and lost I am... How hopeful... And maybe those are even true, maybe... But those are no more the "real me" than the lonely, whining, dissatisfied, pathetic *putz* who pesters you constantly with his inconvenient love.

I swear I've always thought that the internal me was the "real me" and this guy—the one in the world, the one just "doing things" was...I don't know...a facsimile. Not important. Just "the guy out there doing things"...

But now...I mean, Jesus, if I'm *that* guy, that *external* guy—just the sum total of the shit I *do*—then Christ, I just want to scrape out what's left of my heart with a grapefruit spoon... Because it's what you DO that matters, right? That's actually what I've always liked best about Jewish theology. No sinning in your heart. No being punished for your thoughts. It's actions! Not what you say, or think, or *feel*, but what you DO. And if the real me is this guy, this *schmuck* who just wanders through the world bothering people... Then I am so royally fucked I don't know what to do.

ELLA. Vanya, I'm so sorry that—

VANYA. Yeah, I'm just gonna... *(Indicates going.)* you know...

    He leaves...

ELLA. I hope you're enjoying this...because it's no picnic up here...

3.3 A Pair

Pickles enters. She has her hands behind her back...

PICKLES. Hey.

ELLA. Oh, hey.

PICKLES. Hi...

ELLA. What's going on?

PICKLES. I have something for you.

ELLA. For me?

PICKLES. Yeah.

ELLA. Really?

PICKLES. Yep. You want it?

ELLA. Umm...sure.

PICKLES. Close your eyes.

ELLA. Ummm...okay.

> *She does. Pickles reveals her hands with hand-made hand puppets on them. One looks a bit like Ella, one a bit like Pickles.*

PICKLES. You can open your eyes now.

> *She does.*

ELLA. Wow.

PICKLES. This is Waffles. *(As Waffles.)* Hi, Ella. *(As herself.)* And this is Miss Pum-Pum. *(As Pum-Pum.)* Hello, Ella.

ELLA. Those are really...*something.* Did you make them?

PICKLES. Yes I did.

ELLA. And they're for me?

PICKLES. *(Quickly clarifying...)* One is.

ELLA. I'm sorry?

PICKLES. One is. And one I'll keep...

ELLA. Oh.

PICKLES. And then…you know… *(With meaning…)* *we'll each have one.*

ELLA. Okay.

PICKLES. If you want one. I mean, if you don't / want

ELLA. No, no, that's great, I love this, it's / very

PICKLES. You don't have to / take one

ELLA. No, it's great, thank you, Pickles. That's lovely.

PICKLES. Okay. Which one do you want?

ELLA. Well, I… You sure you want to give me one? They seem kind of like a pair.

PICKLES. *(With even more meaning…)* They are.

ELLA. *(Tiny beat.)* Oh. Okay. Well, I really like…

PICKLES. *(As Waffles.)* Choose me! Choose me!

ELLA. …Waffles.

PICKLES. Excellent choice. Here you go…

> *Pickles gives Waffles to Ella…*

ELLA. Thank you.

PICKLES. You're welcome.

ELLA. *(As The Goonster.)* See you around Miss Pum-Pum!

PICKLES. *(As Pum-Pum.)* Bye-bye Waffles!

> *Then Waffles gives Pum-Pum a quick little kiss… Pickles abruptly gives Ella a longer kiss on the lips…then suddenly leaves. Beat. Beat… Waffles slowly looks at Ella. Ella looks back…*

ELLA. What?!?

3.4 Don't Say A Word

> *Aster enters abruptly, urgently…*

ASTER. Hey!
ELLA. Ahhrrgh!

60

ASTER. Never a dull moment, huh?

ELLA. A thrill a minute.

ASTER. The thing is…

ELLA. If you say one more word I will walk out that door, out the front door, into the car, out of the car onto a train, buy a one way ticket for anywhere in the universe and you will never, ever, ever see me again and I swear I mean it. One single word… What is it about me?!? Don't answer that!

What is it? *My eyes? My steel blue eyes? The sadness in my eyes? My irony? My long blonde hair? My Nordic cheekbones? My perfect tits? My boredom? My strength? My need? My contempt?* What??? What makes you think I'd be willing to just give up everything and hurl myself into your arms??? Don't answer that! Don't you dare say a word!!!

> *Beat.*

What is it about me that you all find so…*fucking irresistible*?

ASTER. *(Calmly, truthfully, confidently.)* It's your contradictions.

ELLA. Hmm.

> *She suddenly kisses him fuller and deeper and sexier than kisses are supposed to go onstage…and then abruptly stops. Then steps back and slaps him once, really hard, right across the face…*

Maybe you're right.

> *Music. Everyone else suddenly joins them in one fell swoop…*

3.5 Three Things I Hate

PICKLES. This scene is called: Three things I hate

VANYA. Myself.
Others.
Optimists.

PROFESSOR. Vanya.
Bad Art.
Aging.

ELLA. Weakness.

Strength.

All the same-old day-to-day-to-day-to-day-to-day-to-day horseshit.

ASTER. Selfishness.

Stupidity.

Asparagus.

PICKLES. Nicknames.

Narcissists.

Bad things happening to good people.

SONIA. My body.

My face.

The lie of Literature.

BABS. Bullshit.

Humidity.

Lists.

3.6 A Conundrum

Instant shift into the family gathering that the Professor has called...

PROFESSOR. Well, now, thank you all for coming. So... Well, you know...life is a conundrum, isn't it? A conundrum wrapped in a riddle, sautéed in an enigma, and peppered, as it were, with mystery.

BABS. Oh dear.

PROFESSOR. As Euripides so wisely wrote: "Zoy dane ay nye pahnta aftoo pou nomizetaya."

PICKLES. ...aftoo pou...?

PROFESSOR. Life is not always what you think. I believe that is a great truth. Simple, perhaps, and yet profound. Life does not tend to go exactly where you thought it might go when you boldly headed out on the Great Journey.

And needs are needs...

VANYA. Oh, this can't be good.

PROFESSOR. So, as of late…certain ventures, certain ventures of a financial nature…did not perform as we had hoped, and now we find ourselves in a bit of a…well, a bit of a pickle, as it were…a financially precarious pickle.

PICKLES. Hey! Twinsies!

They all look at her…

I'm a financially precarious pickle.

VANYA. Please…!

PICKLES. Sorry.

PROFESSOR. Well, not to put too fine a point on it—we need money, and the only certain place to get it is to…sell this house and use the proceeds to pay off some debts and get a leg up and see if we can't…right our fiscal ship, as it were.

SONIA.	ASTER.	BABS.
I'm sorry?	Are you kidding?	Wow.

PROFESSOR. I know it won't be uncomplicated, but a house like this, what with the garden and the outbuildings and all, is worth quite a pretty penny these days, and there may well be ways we could all benefit / from making smart decisions

VANYA. You're not the sun!

PROFESSOR. I'm sorry…what?!?!

VANYA. YOU. ARE NOT. THE FUCKING. SUN! The world / does not revolve

SONIA. Uncle Vanya, please don't…

VANYA. around you and your fucking needs and your fucking predicaments and your fucking fucking fucking fucking fucking PICKLES!

PROFESSOR. You are insane. You won't / even do me the simple

ELLA. *(Interrupting.)* I told you this was not the time…

VANYA. *(Interrupting, with Ella.)* Yes, I think that's right. I think I must be insane, I think I must be hallucinating because it seems to me that you just told us that you NEED MONEY and therefore plan to sell a house that DOES NOT BELONG TO YOU to raise money for… I mean… WHAT??? This is Sonia's house! Hers, not

63

yours, you fucking moron! Hers! She and I have been working our asses off for years and years and years, paying the mortgage, and keeping this house up without the slightest help / from you

PROFESSOR. Now that's enough…!

> *Vanya is starting to lose it. A lifetime of rage and frustration and sadness and shattered things come pouring out all at once…a huge amount of feeling trying to get out of a bottle with not nearly a wide enough mouth…*

VANYA. Enough?!? That's not NEARLY ENOUGH! How about this: I fucking hate you and everything you are and everything you do and everything you think and…and… Wait! Wait! Wait right here…

> *He runs off…*

PROFESSOR. I have never in my life / seen such an…infantile…

SONIA. He doesn't mean it, things have been very tight and we've been working so hard to make ends meet, and he's been very upset / recently, and I

ELLA. Where do you think he went?

BABS. Probably to get my gun and shoot him in the face.

ELLA. Ha ha, very funny.

PROFESSOR. I wouldn't / put it past him. Did you see his eyes?

ASTER. *(To Babs. While they are talking they're hardly paying attention to their own conversation, but trying to listen to the Professor and Ella and clock Vanya…)* You have a gun?

BABS. Oh, just a little one…

ASTER. Why do you have a gun?

BABS. You're going to come over at three A.M. and shoot the raccoons…or cat burglars?

ASTER. Cat burglars? What, in little black masks?

BABS. No, those are the raccoons…

PROFESSOR. *(This continues straight on from the previous line…)* They went all goggly. I mean, for God's sake, I was simply talking about a possible—

ELLA. Don't. Not again. Let it go…

PROFESSOR. A person can't talk? A person can't—

Vanya comes running back in, a small gun in hand...!

VANYA. I HOPE YOU ROT IN HELL!

Vanya shoots at the Professor, in full expectation of killing or at least wounding him. There are four bullets in the gun and some empty clicks as well. While he shoots people scream, duck, etc. etc. When he is done shooting, everyone just kinds of holds where they are as the Professor realizes that he has not been hit by even one of the bullets. He is totally fine...

PROFESSOR. *(Stunned, amazed, aghast...)* You missed...!

VANYA. *(Stunned, amazed, aghast...)* I missed. I fucking missed...

PROFESSOR. *(Stunned, amazed, aghast...)* You just tried to kill me.

VANYA. *(Stunned, amazed, aghast...)* Yeah.

PROFESSOR. Well you failed! Like everything you've ever done, you pathetic fuck!

ELLA. Robbie, Robbie...

PROFESSOR. We will leave here forever!

He starts storming out. This line continues all the way off-stage...

I have never... I can't believe... / What the fuck is the world coming to when...when...

He leaves with Ella right behind him...

ELLA. Are you all right? Are sure you're all right...?

SONIA. Oh, Uncle Vanya...

She leaves.

Beat.

PICKLES. *(Utterly amazed.)* Oh my God, that just happened. That just really happened.

VANYA. Shut up...

PICKLES. All right...

She sits down in a corner somewhere...

BABS. Look at me. *(Forceful. No bullshit at all.)* Look at me!

VANYA. *(Slowly looking at her.)* Yes?

BABS. Are you okay now? Or do I need to go call someone right now?

VANYA. No. I'm fine.

> *Quick serious beat.*

I'm *fine*.

BABS. Okay. Okay.

> *She steps aside, satisfied for the moment...*

ASTER. Those were real bullets, right?

BABS. Yeah.

VANYA. Yeah.

ASTER. Wow. You missed him three times. And you were standing pretty damn close.

VANYA. Yeah.

ASTER. I think you're the one who dodged a bullet, my friend.

VANYA. Yeah.

ASTER. I...I need a drink. Would anyone like a drink?

VANYA.	PICKLES.	BABS.
Yeah.	Sure	Absolutely.

> *Aster leaves. It's now just Vanya and Babs. Vanya is maybe beginning to realize the reality of what he just did...and didn't do... Beat.*

BABS. I thought I had maybe seen all the things I was going to see, you know. I thought my highlight reel might be full, but this... I love you, Vanya. I always have. You are smart as a whip and can talk me and pretty much anyone else in circles...you know so much about so many things... But, I swear, you don't seem to understand a blessed thing about anything that really matters in the world, and that's the God's honest truth.

VANYA. Yeah.

BABS. You can't just go and shoot at someone because he disappoints you...

VANYA. Yeah.

BABS. Or because he reminds you how much you disappoint yourself.

VANYA. Yeah.

BABS. Or because you really want to sleep with his wife. Even if you actually do love his wife…

VANYA. Yeah.

BABS. I'm so, so, so sorry you're hurting, Vanya, but you've really gotta…you know…*get it together.*

VANYA. Yeah.

BABS. Yeah.

     Beat…

VANYA. How?

     Beat…

Life sucks.

BABS. Sometimes.

VANYA. Life fucking sucks.

BABS. Yes, sometimes.

VANYA. Not all the times?

BABS. No. Not all the times.

VANYA. Oh. Okay.

     Beat.

BABS. *(To us.)* End of Act Three

End of Act Three

ACT FOUR: AFTERMATH

4.0 The Gratitudes

Babs doesn't leave. She just turns to us and starts talking...
Before too long Sonia wanders on unseen by Babs and listens
to most of this...

BABS. So, yeah, well...my Zadie Oscar died in a plane crash when I
was thirteen. (Don't worry, I have a point...) He was born in Poltava,
in the Ukraine, and came over here with his four younger brothers and
actually managed to get rich. A hot dog cart, then a burger shack, then
a steakhouse. Oscar's. Very fancy. The American Dream made good...
He was a character, as they say. Quite a natty dresser, slicked-back
hair, pencil-thin mustache. He was also, apparently, quite the gam-
bler, drinker, and womanizer, but I didn't know any of that then. To
me he was "Zadie Oscar," the life of the party who would slip a five-
dollar bill into your palm when Bubbe Margie wasn't looking. It
always seemed to me he knew some secret that no one else knew
that made him awfully happy. I remember asking my mother about
it all the way back then. She told me he was "a life-eater," a particular type of person. That he ate life the way the rest of us ate latkes...
could never get enough, could never have his fill...
And speaking of eating, here's my point: Before every family meal I
can ever remember eating with him, we did what he called, with
grave seriousness, The Gratitudes. Everyone at the table—family,
strangers, everyone, young and old—had to take a moment and say
what they were grateful for *at that moment*. Kind of like Grace, but
without God. Or holding hands...
And sometimes it was just simple little things like a raise, or finding
a dollar in the gutter, or a good knish... But often someone would...
go deep. And things would come out. *Real* things. About other
people at the table...or those lost to us. I remember a lot of tears,
but also lots of laughing.

But it was always *real*. *Real* gratitude. An odd kind of secular prayer or or or humble appreciation for the miracle of making it through another day, and having something good to eat at the end of it, and someone to eat it with.

I still say them. Mostly to myself, but I say them.

Every meal. Every day.

So, here's my point:

4.1 Not the Answer...

SONIA. *(Suddenly, from elsewhere onstage...)* Life sucks.

BABS. *(Putting out her arms for a hug.)* Oh, c'mere.

SONIA. Life *sucks*.

BABS. *(About the shooting...)* I know, I know...

SONIA. *(Confused...)* Oh...what?

BABS. I can't believe it either. I never thought he'd actually do anything as...as insanely extreme as that.

SONIA. Oh. Oh, yeah, totally...

BABS. Oh, wait, is that not what...?

SONIA. No no no, no, yeah, that, that was...ummm...

BABS. What's going on, honey?

SONIA. Oh...*nothing*. It's just...well...I just...

BABS. Oh shit.

SONIA. What?!

BABS. Really?

SONIA. What?

BABS. The *doctor*?

SONIA. *(Incredulous.)* Is it really / *that* obvious?!?

BABS. Of course.

SONIA. Oh, God.

BABS. You're not alone. I know he's *practically irresistible*, in all his...*graying patrician aloofness...*

69

SONIA. I know!

BABS. I'm sorry you're hurting...

SONIA. It's awful. I shake inside when I see him. My insides just go...

She does a weird little shaking action...

I literally have to restrain myself to not just...reach out and grab him. And just...hold him. Or *stroke him...*

BABS. Oh, dear.

SONIA. I only hear about half of what he says because I'm just watching his lips, and picturing him just—oh, God, is it okay that I'm telling you this?

BABS. Get it out! No judgment here, believe me.

SONIA. I *want* him! And he *needs* me. And if he won't love me back I don't know if I will survive it. I think I might just...just...

BABS. No, you won't. You'll survive it. I know it doesn't feel that way, but—

SONIA. How do you know?

BABS. I *know.*

SONIA. Oh, please don't tell me I'm young, or when you were / my age

BABS. *(With both clarity and code...)* When I was your age I felt just what you're feeling! *Precisely* what you're feeling...

SONIA. What I'm feeling— *(Shockingly putting it together...)* Wait, what?

BABS. *(With fuller meaning...)* Because I know he's practically ir- resistible. *(Landing this idea with great clarity...)* And always has been...

SONIA. Wait...what are you saying?

BABS. I'm saying *I know what you're feeling.* But *exactly...*
You know the doctor moved here when he was maybe nine or ten and he and Vanya have been friends forever. Vanya followed him around like his own private superhero: "Nature-Boy" or whatever. Oh, you should have seen Aster back then. So cute. So *serious...*

SONIA. Wait, are you really telling me...?

BABS. *(Going right on...)* Just listen. One day when he was fifteen or sixteen he was just hanging around the house, waiting for Vanya,

70

who was inevitably late for everything—he had an innate knack for pissing people off, even back then—and, well, I don't remember exactly but suddenly we were talking about...*life*. A real talk. About the environment and nature and...The Way Things Are, and suddenly Boom! There it was. I was...*interested.*

I started noticing when he was around and found ways to...engage him, spend time in odd little ways...and show him a little flash of something or make a just-barely-off-color comment without seeming to notice... Believe me, putting sex in the room for a sixteen-year-old boy is no great challenge...

SONIA. I can't believe I'm even hearing this...

BABS. Okay, well, this is getting long. So...I seduced him. He thought he seduced me. He probably *still* thinks that. Hell, knowing him he probably still feels bad about it, feels like he took advantage of me, but I was the one doing the taking. Mostly...

SONIA. Oh, my God...

BABS. I'm not saying it was right. What I did. But...life is for living, right? Not running away from. And life just seemed to want this to happen...

SONIA. Why are you telling me this? And why haven't you ever told me before?

BABS. You know what the doctor is...? He's a *human being.* A flawed, fabulous, broken, ridiculous *human being.* And I know you think he is *it*, the One, the Thing That Could Make Everything Better, *but that is almost always a lie.* And with him...*I know it is.* I know it's nearly impossible to hear what I'm saying, but...I'm *right. Move on.* The Doctor Is Not The Answer.

SONIA. Then...what happens to all that love? To everything I feel...?

BABS. It will move forward. Into the world... I know it's hard to see when you're in the middle of it, but this is just a part of the... shape of things. *Have a little faith.* Have a little gratitude for all the things you've got and...*move on...*

SONIA. But Pickles always says...

BABS. She's wrong. I love her dearly, but...*consider the source.* Move on... Move *forward.* Move *further into life.*

SONIA. Wow…

Vanya enters…

BABS. Hey. How are you?

VANYA. I have one more thing to tell them. Can I have the room…?

BABS. Sure…

SONIA. *(To Vanya.)* Are you / okay?

VANYA. *(To Sonia, a tad abrupt.)* I'm fine.

SONIA. Okay.

BABS. Vanya.

VANYA. Yeah?

BABS. Don't do anything stupid.

VANYA. No more than usual.

BABS. Okay, then…

Sonia and Babs exit.

4.2 Joy

VANYA. *(Directly to us.)* The Joy is Gone. Gone. Oooooops. Bye-bye "Joy," I hardly knew thee… She used to come and go regularly, good old "Joy." Gone for the holidays. Here one odd, rainy morning for a few hours; away for a month; back during nearly all of *Infinite Jest*; gone for my birthday month; back for a crisp weekend in October… Fleeting little visits after good meals or a nice chat with an old chum or whatever, but now… Done. No more Joy. Makes getting out of bed on cold mornings nearly *inconceivable.*

Chilly, lonely breakfasts might be the worst first-world problem ever.

Quick beat…

So, what's the worst, most painful thing about your life that makes the thought of more endless, impossible days *approximately tragic*? Oh right, how stupid, you can't answer that. You're all here with other people… And while you might think about telling a group of *total strangers* about the deepest, hardest part of your life, you can't admit it in front of Michael. Or Megan. Or Greg and Susie. Or Simone.

Or Mrs. Finkelstein. Because you had dinner with them an hour ago and you never told them that three mornings a week you wake up in despair. Or that if you had to sum up your life in one word it would be...*disappointed*. Or *lost*. Or...

Or maybe it's just me. Maybe you're all fine, and...Tom and Tim and Terrence and Tabitha and Tariq and Tamisha and Tong Il Han already know everything there is to know about you...

Shit. Life life life, huh? Can't live with it, can't...

4.3 Everything

Aster enters...

ASTER. Hey.

VANYA. Hey.

ASTER. So... What's going on here, pal?

VANYA. Isn't it...painfully obvious?

ASTER. No. So tell me: What's really wrong?

VANYA. *Everything.*

ASTER. Wow. That's a lot...

VANYA. Yeah. But there it is. I've been taking a good hard look at my life and

ASTER. ...yeah?

VANYA. as far as I can tell I've done everything wrong.

ASTER. *Everything?*

VANYA. I think so. I think *everything*...

ASTER. Not *everything*.

VANYA. Yeah, I think so...

ASTER. C'mon, you can't have done *everything* wrong.

VANYA. Everything that *matters*. Everything *real*... Yeah, fucking *everything*.

Quick beat...small change of tone and energy...

73

ASTER. And therefore…?

VANYA. What?

ASTER. And therefore…???

VANYA. I heard you, I just don't know / what you

ASTER. "And therefore, my dear Doctor, I am going to do X…or Y…or Z to change my life."

Beat. Nothing…

"And *therefore*, my dear old friend, having now finally fully realized the depth of the wrongness of my choices over the past X many years, I now resolve to Y. Or Z. Or W." Or some fucking thing, because I gotta tell you, Vanya, with all due love and respect and genuine affection in the world, there is a limit to the amount of…self-indulgent angst-y wallowing even your nearest and dearest can endure if you don't…you know…at least try to DO SOMETHING / ABOUT IT!

VANYA. What?! What am I supposed to / do? What the hell…

ASTER. *(Entirely improvised…)* Move! Quit your job! Study Egyptian basket weaving or or or Hindu macramé. Buy a bike. Learn to bake. Sell all your belongings on eBay and move to Kenosha, Wisconsin, or East Jabip or outer fucking Mongolia! But, Heavens to Murgatroyd, man, IF YOU DON'T LIKE YOUR LIFE, THEN FUCKING DO SOMETHING / TO MAKE IT BETTER!

VANYA. I'VE TRIED! You think I haven't tried All Those Things? Trips and books and online dating and diets and exercise plans. Gyms rejoice when they see me coming because they know I'll pay their exorbitant fees and go exactly three times before I…get a cold or pull something in my groin or just…you know…*stop going*! Lose energy. Lose momentum. Lose…lose…*lose*…

ASTER. …what?

VANYA. …*belief*. Okay?! BELIEF!!! Lose the motherfucking BELIEF that I will ever really *change*, that I will ever be anything other than the over-educated, under-motivated, grumpy, *kvetching shithead* you see before you, trapped in the endless cycle of his own failure and…lack of will, and and and…

ASTER. Give them back.

VANYA. What?

74

ASTER. Give them back. Now.

VANYA. I don't know / what you're

ASTER. Don't fuck me around on this, they're prescription pills, you don't have one, I'm your friend, they'll assume I gave them to you and it will be horribly bad for me, so if you really are thinking of doing the stupidest, stupidest, stupidest, stupidest, STUPIDEST fucking thing you could ever do, you are going to need to steal a car and drive off a cliff or or or spontaneously combust or somefuckingthing, but you are NOT going to do it with pills that can be traced back to me, and you are not going to do it at all because it is ridiculous and insane and there are those of us who actually love you, impossible as you are, and would miss your troll-ish self, so give me back both bottles… Take a long hot bath or go for a walk or eat a box of Nutty Buddys or something, and, you know…buck up.

Buck the fuck up and get on with living. This is your ONE LIFE, this is *it*, this is all you get, EVER. This is not a dress rehearsal for some stupid fucking play or a a a rough draft of that novel you started, the the the *Daily Turtle* or—

VANYA. *The Quotidian Tortoise!*

ASTER. Whatever! This is not some placeholder for life. This is it! This is YOUR ONE, OWN, ONLY little life. And you—and *only* you—can make it better.

Surely you can do that. And I will NOT quit calling you Shirley. So deal with that, too, bucko.

     It has landed, but not fully. Not well enough. On to step two…

(Calling offstage…) Hey, can you all come out here, please…!

4.4 What, Am I Supposed to Feel Sorry for You?

Suddenly the rest of the cast appear en masse and move into positions for the scene that is about to take place. Someone places a chair downstage center facing upstage, for Vanya. The rest gather upstage.

VANYA. Oh, God. This can't be good…

ASTER. It's for your own good. This is called "What, am I supposed to feel sorry for you?" Ready?

VANYA. As I'll ever be…

ASTER. Okay then…

VANYA. Let the games begin…

PICKLES. I'll go first.

What, am I supposed to feel sorry for you?

My life is just *ridiculous*. Everyone calls me *Pickles*. And has forever. But my real name is Penelope. Penelope Pickford Grunen. My mom wanted me to be a myth…or a movie star… Not a Pickles.

I wanted to be a mom. I wanted to be a great artist and make those huge paintings that fill whole walls in museums, not just…stupid wall hangings…and sock puppets and oven mitts to sell at bake sales…but none of that happened. I live above a garage, I lost the only woman I ever loved, I dropped out of life, and I became…a Pickles.

ELLA. What, am I supposed to feel sorry for you?

I'm unhappy, too, you know. And I've done all the things I was told would make me happy! I *read*, I *studied*, I went to church *and* therapy. I have a BA from Amherst, a Masters from Duke, and a PhD from Northwestern. And I fell head over heels for this brilliant professor; the smartest one, the one I should never have been able to get, and I got him… I got it all…

And none of it has made me happy.

So, here I am with a half-finished book on phenomenology no human being would ever want to read, a seriously floundering marriage, $173,000 in student loans, and most of the time I just feel lost…just… *irretrievably lost.*

ASTER. What, am I supposed to feel sorry for you?
I work my ass off! At my job...and for the *world*! I work and work and stress and contribute and volunteer for causes, and run 5k's and 10k's for This Disease and That Disaster...and do you know why? Do you? Because if I allowed myself to fully live in relation to how *comprehensively fucked* everything is, I wouldn't get out of bed in the mornings. So I drink too much and work out too much and sleep with the wrong people and compulsively try to fix everything so I just...won't think about anything. *Ever.*
That's no way to live.

VANYA. But you just said—...!

ASTER. I know what I said! Why do you think I want you to get your shit together? Figure it out and send me a fucking map...

PROFESSOR. So, what, am I supposed to feel sorry for you?
I'm on the downhill slope. Of my life. Of my whole fucking *life*. My health is...*not so good*, and will not get any better, it seems, so it's all just downhill from here. Which just seems...shocking, and horrible, and utterly unfair. Like someone somewhere has gotten something terribly wrong.
Of course we all know death is coming *eventually*, but knowing it *theoretically* is one thing, and actually feeling it...*slowly encroaching*...well that's another thing altogether, and...and...and it's scaring the shit out of me, if you want to know the truth. It's scaring the fucking shit out of me.

SONIA. What, am I supposed to feel sorry for you?
Because I do! I do, I really do. I never say it, and I don't even always feel it, but not a day goes by that I don't love you and want you to be...well, not even *happy*, necessarily, but...happy-ish. Not in pain. Not so sad and frustrated and and and...ferociously *un*-happy when I think you could be...just incredible. I really do. I just really think you could be this incredible person in the world. So, yes, I feel sorry for you, but not as sorry as I would be for me if I had to go through the rest of my life without you.

BABS. What, am I supposed to feel sorry for you?
Vanya. *Bubbie... Life* is just *life*. Life is just exactly life, you know that, right? And we should be grateful every day. We can breathe in and out. We have food and friends and people who love us. We've

been given this ridiculous gift, and yet…we find the most extraordinary ways to fuck it all up. But I don't think it has to be as hard as we make it, I really, really don't.

Spoiler alert: Most of us won't get everything we want.

Most of us won't ever find our *bashert*…

Bad things will happen to good people. And, worse maybe—*visa versa*. And yet…I'm trying to live every day like my grandfather—my Zadie Oscar—and eat every morsel of Life I can before I'm through. As my dear friend Dr. Aster would say… Why not? Why the fuck not?

4.5 Imagine

That scene is now over. Lights and/or sound shift. They all just sit there…

VANYA. Well, fuck.

    He goes to the Professor.

Robert, I'm sorry.

PROFESSOR. *(Prompting him for specifics…)* For what…?

VANYA. *(Trying…)* I'm sorry… I'm sorry…

PROFESSOR. Yes…?

VANYA. That I tried to kill you. I'm sorry that I tried to kill you. All right?

    Ella starts laughing, quietly, uncontrollably…

PROFESSOR. Forget it. It's past. You're not going to try again, are you?

VANYA. No.

PROFESSOR. All right then. Let's move on.

VANYA. Thank you. I'm an idiot…

PROFESSOR. Yes, well…

ELLA. *(Stopping him gently, but firmly.)* Robert…

VANYA. Excellent.

    Beat…

Yeah, okay, so… *(To actors and audience.)* Sorry everyone. Sorry for the…you know…*shooting*…and *kvetching*…and whatnot.

PICKLES. That's okay.

VANYA. The thing is…

> *He finds it hard to go on…*

BABS. …yeah?

VANYA. The thing is…

ASTER. …what is it, pal?

BABS. Breathe…

VANYA. Okay, look, so, here's the thing…I think it was my third or maybe my fourth therapist who said there is only one question in life you ever really need to ask…or *answer*… And that is: "What Do You Want?"

ASTER. It's a good question.

BABS. It's a great question.

PICKLES. It's a hard question.

ELLA. It's an impossible question.

SONIA. It's an easy question…

PROFESSOR. It's the quintessential question, actually…

VANYA. So, you know what I really, really want, when all is said and done? Under all the ridiculous moaning and and and…*tsuris*… you know what I really want?

PICKLES. What?

VANYA. I want to be *loved*…by *everybody*…*all the time*…*no matter what*.

ASTER.	BABS.	PROFESSOR.
That can't happen…	Not gonna happen…	That's utterly specious…

PICKLES. That's not possible.

VANYA. *Since when does that matter?* We want what we want no matter why we want it. The last thing that makes any difference is how much *sense* it makes.

PICKLES.	ELLA.	ASTER.
For sure…	True.	Yeah, that's fair…

VANYA. And the truth is…I want everyone I meet to love me, totally and entirely, day in and day out, just because *I'm me*. I want to be loved, *just as I am, on my own terms, by everyone, all the time.* *That's* what I want.

PICKLES. But…you can't have that.

VANYA. I know. *That's* why life sucks.

SONIA. No it doesn't.

VANYA. Yes it does.

SONIA. No, it doesn't.

VANYA. Yes…it does.

SONIA. Well I don't think it does.

VANYA. Well, you're wrong.

SONIA. No, I'm not. I don't think life sucks.

PROFESSOR. I think it kind of does.

ELLA. I don't. I *don't*. I just SO don't want that to be true…

BABS. Amen…

PICKLES. I don't think life sucks. *I* might suck sometimes, but Life doesn't suck…

SONIA. Well, I don't think life sucks. I don't. I really don't. And I don't think Pickles sucks, and I don't think my ridiculous Uncle Vanya sucks and…and…and I don't even think I suck.

ASTER. You *don't*.

SONIA. I just think life is… I think life is just… Life is… I guess I'm not really sure. *(Directly to the audience.)* What do *you* think? Seriously…what do you think???

> The whole cast looks out at the audience and waits to hear what they have to say. Maybe they say things. Maybe they say nothing. The cast listens and maybe responds. After some time has passed, at the right moment…

VANYA or SONIA. End of play.

> *Lights out.*

End of Play

PROPERTY LIST

(Use this space to create props lists for your production)

SOUND EFFECTS
(Use this space to create sound effects lists for your production)